국제토셀위원회

TOSEL®

실전문제집

개정판

BASIC

최신 기출 경향반영 실전모의고사 수록
국제토셀위원회 공식교재

CONTENTS

Actual Test 1 page 09

Actual Test 2 page 34

Actual Test 3 page 59

Actual Test 4 page 84

Actual Test 5 page 109

Appendix (Vocabulary) page 135

OMR 카드

정답 및 해설 별책

About this book

1 Actual Test

토셀 최신 유형을 반영하여
실전 모의고사를 5회 실었습니다.
수험자들의 토셀 시험 대비 및
적응력 향상에 도움이 됩니다.

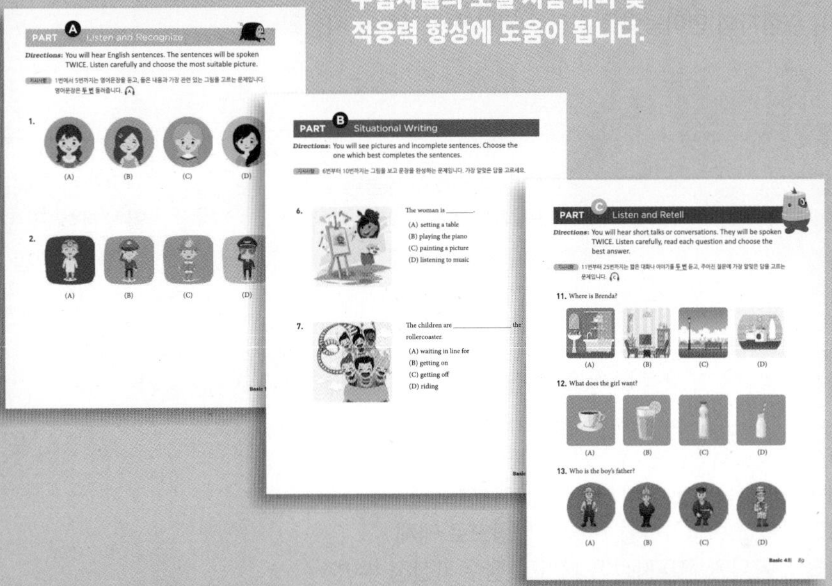

2 Appendix

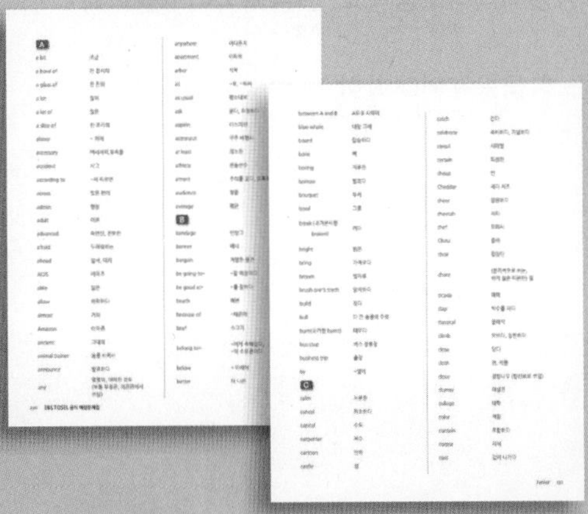

필수 어휘를 포함해 모의고사
빈출 어휘 목록을 수록했습니다.
평소 어휘 정리뿐만 아니라
시험 직전 대비용으로 활용 가능합니다.

3 Answer

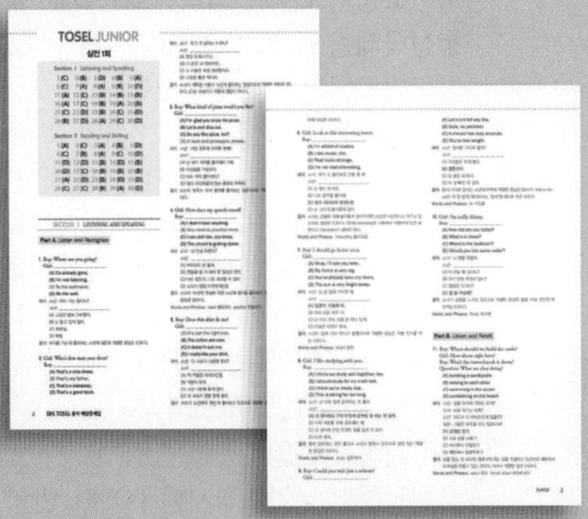

자세한 해설과 문제 풀이로
오답 확인 및 시험 대비를 위한 정리가 가능합니다.

About TOSEL® — TOSEL에 대하여

TOSEL은 각급 학교 교과과정과 연령별 인지단계를 고려하여 단계별 난이도와 문항으로
영어 숙달 정도를 측정하는 영어 사용자 중심의 맞춤식 영어능력인증 시험제도입니다.
평가유형에 따른 개인별 장점과 단점을 파악하고, 개인별 영어학습 방향을 제시하는 성적분석자료를 제공하여
영어능력 종합검진 서비스를 제공함으로써 영어 사용자인 소비자와
영어능력 평가를 토대로 영어교육을 담당하는 교사 및 기관 인사관리자인 공급자를
모두 만족시키는 영어능력인증 평가입니다.

TOSEL은 인지적-학문적 언어 사용의 유칭성 (Cognitive-Academic Language Proficiency, CALP)과
기본적-개인적 의사소통능력 (Basic Interpersonal Communication Skill, BICS)을
엄밀히 구분하여 수험자의 언어능력을 가장 친밀하게 평가하는 시험입니다.

대상	목적	용도
유아, 초, 중, 고등학생, 대학생 및 직장인 등 성인	한국인의 영어구사능력 증진과 비영어권 국가의 영어 사용자의 영어구사능력 증진	실질적인 영어구사능력 평가 + 입학전형 및 인재선발 등에 활용 및 직무역량별 인재 배치

연혁

2002.02	국제토셀위원회 창설 (수능출제위원역임 전국대학 영어전공교수진 중심)
2004.09	TOSEL 고려대학교 국제어학원 공동인증시험 실시
2006.04	EBS 한국교육방송공사 주관기관 참여
2006.05	민족사관고등학교 입학전형에 반영
2008.12	고려대학교 편입학시험 TOSEL 유형으로 대체
2009.01	서울시 공무원 근무평정에 TOSEL 점수 가산점 부여
2009.01	전국 대부분 외고, 자사고 입학전형에 TOSEL 반영 (한영외국어고등학교, 한일고등학교, 고양외국어고등학교, 과천외국어고등학교, 김포외국어고등학교, 명지외국어고등학교, 부산국제외국어고등학교, 부일외국어 고등학교, 성남외국어고등학교, 인천외국어고등학교, 전북외국어고등학교, 대전외국어고등학교, 청주외국어고등학교, 강원외국어고등학교, 전남외국어고등학교)
2009.12	청심국제중 • 고등학교 입학전형 TOSEL 반영
2009.12	한국외국어교육학회, 팬코리아영어교육학회, 한국음성학회, 한국응용언어학회 TOSEL 인증
2010.03	고려대학교, TOSEL 출제기관 및 공동 인증기관으로 참여
2010.07	경찰청 공무원 임용 TOSEL 성적 가산점 부여
2014.04	전국 200개 초등학교 단체 응시 실시
2017.03	중앙일보 주관기관 참여
2018.11	관공서, 대기업 등 100여 개 기관에서 TOSEL 반영
2019.06	미얀마 TOSEL 도입 발족식 베트남 TOSEL 도입 협약식
2019.11	고려대학교 편입학전형 반영
2020.06	국토교통부 국가자격시험 TOSEL 반영
2021.07	소방청 간부후보생 선발시험 TOSEL 반영
2021.11	고려대학교 공과대학 기계학습 • 빅데이터 연구원 AI 연구 협약
2022.05	AI 영어학습 플랫폼 TOSEL Lab 공개
2023.11	고려대학교 경영대학 전국 고등학생 대상 정기캠퍼스 투어 프로그램 후원기관 참여
2024.01	제1회 TOSEL VOCA 올림피아드 실시
2024.03	고려대학교 미래교육원 TOSEL 전문가과정 개설

About TOSEL® — TOSEL에 대하여

"Test of Skills in the English Language"

TOSEL은 비영어권 국가의 영어 사용자를 대상으로 영어구사능력을 측정하여 그 결과를 공식 인증하는 영어능력인증 시험제도입니다.

영어 사용자 중심의 맞춤식 영어능력 인증 시험제도

맞춤식 평가

획일적인 평가에서 세분화된 평가로의 전환

TOSEL은 응시자의 연령별 인지단계에 따라 별도의 문항과 난이도를 적용하여 평가함으로써 평가의 목적과 용도에 적합한 평가 시스템을 구축하였습니다.

공정성과 신뢰성 확보

국제토셀위원회의 역할

TOSEL은 고려대학교가 출제 및 인증기관으로 참여하였고 대학입학수학능력시험 출제위원 교수들이 중심이 된 국제토셀위원회가 주관하여 사회적 공정성과 신뢰성을 확보한 평가 제도입니다.

수입대체 효과

외화유출 차단 및 국위선양

TOSEL은 해외시험응시로 인한 외화의 유출을 막는 수입대체의 효과를 기대할 수 있습니다. TOSEL의 문항과 시험제도는 비영어권 국가에 수출하여 국위선양에 기여하고 있습니다.

TOSEL에 관한 자세한 설명은 QR코드 속 영상을 참조해 주세요.

Evaluation — 평가

평가의 기본원칙

TOSEL은 PBT(Paper Based Test)를 통하여 간접평가와 직접평가를 모두 시행합니다.

TOSEL은 언어의 네 가지 요소인 **읽기, 듣기, 말하기, 쓰기 영역을 모두 평가합니다.**

Reading 읽기	모든 레벨의 읽기 영역은 직접 평가 방식으로 측정합니다.
Listening 듣기	모든 레벨의 듣기 영역은 직접 평가 방식으로 측정합니다.
Writing 쓰기	모든 레벨의 쓰기 영역은 간접 평가 방식으로 측정합니다.
Speaking 말하기	모든 레벨의 말하기 영역은 간접 평가 방식으로 측정합니다.

TOSEL은 연령별 인지단계를 고려하여 **아래와 같이 7단계로 나누어 평가합니다.**

1 단계	TOSEL® COCOON	5~7세의 미취학 아동
2 단계	TOSEL® Pre-STARTER	초등학교 1~2학년
3 단계	TOSEL® STARTER	초등학교 3~4학년
4 단계	TOSEL® BASIC	초등학교 5~6학년
5 단계	TOSEL® JUNIOR	중학생
6 단계	TOSEL® HIGH JUNIOR	고등학생
7 단계	TOSEL® ADVANCED	대학생 및 성인

Grade Report

성적표 및 인증서

고도화 성적표: 응시자 개인별 최적화 AI 정밀진단

20여년간 축적된 약 100만명 이상의 엄선된 응시자 빅데이터를 TOSEL AI로 분석 · 진단한 개인별 성적자료

전국 단위 연령, 레벨 통계자료를 활용하여 보다 정밀한 성취 수준 판별
파트별 강/약점, 영역별 역량, 8가지 지능, 단어 수준 등을 비교 및 분석하여 폭넓은 학습 진단
오답 문항 유형별 심층 분석 자료 및 솔루션으로 학습 방향 제시, TOSEL과 수능 및 교과학습 성취기준과의 연계
모바일 기기 지원 - UX/UI 개선, 반응형 웹페이지로 구현되어 태블릿, 휴대폰, PC 등 다양한 기기 환경에서 접근 가능

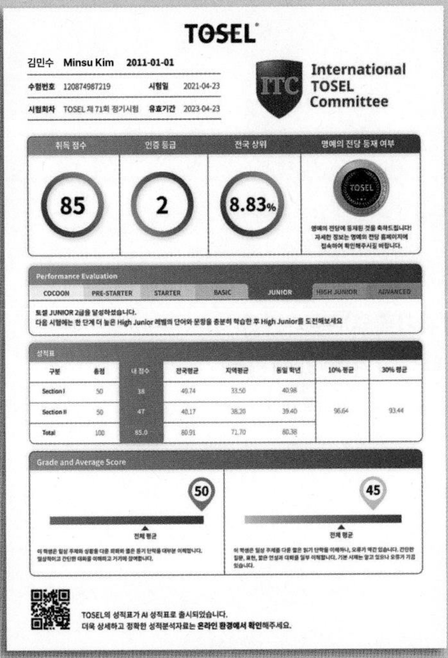

기본 제공 성적표

고도화 성적표 (일부 유료)

단체 성적 분석 자료

단체 및 기관 대상

- 레벨별 평균성적추이, 학생분포
  섹션 및 영역별 평균 점수, 표준편차

TOSEL Lab 지정교육기관 대상 추가 제공

- 원생 별 취약영역 분석 및 보강방안 제시
- TOSEL수험심리척도를 바탕으로 학생의 응답 특이성을
  파악하여 코칭 방안 제시
- 전국 및 지역 단위 종합적 비교분석
  (레벨/유형별 응시자 연령 및 규모, 최고득점 등)

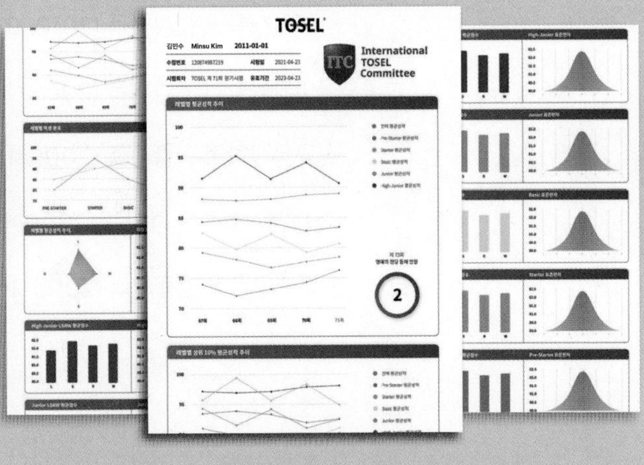

'토셀 명예의 전당' 등재

특별시, 광역시, 도 별 **1등 선발**
(7개시 9개도 **1등 선발**)

*홈페이지 로그인 - 시험결과 - 명예의 전당에서
해당자 등재 증명서 출력 가능

'학업성취기록부'에 토셀 인증등급 기재

개인별 **'학업성취기록부' 평생 발급**
진학과 취업을 대비한 **필수 스펙관리**

영어능력 학업성취기록부

Name In full : 나토셀 Date of birth : 2000-03-09

응시회차	날짜	응시레벨	인증취득사항
토셀 제 53회 정기시험	2016-08-20	HIGH JUNIOR	1등급
토셀 제 46회 정기시험	2015-02-28	JUNIOR	1등급
토셀 제 43회 정기시험	2014-06-28	JUNIOR	3등급
토셀 제 39회 정기시험	2013-08-24	BASIC	3등급

국제토셀위원회는 나토셀(NAH TO SEL) 학생의 학업성취기록을 상기와 같이 인증합니다.

International TOSEL Committee
국제토셀위원회

인증서

대한민국 초,중,고등학생의 영어숙달능력 평가 결과 공식인증

고려대학교 인증획득 (2010. 03)

한국외국어교육학회 인증획득 (2009. 12)

한국음성학회 인증획득 (2009. 12)

한국응용언어학회 인증획득 (2009. 11)

팬코리아영어교육학회 인증획득 (2009. 10)

International TOSEL Committee TOSEL®

Certificate of Achievement

This certificate is awarded to the following person
for their achievement in the

TOSEL® Advanced Test

grade 1

Republic of Korea
88th TOSEL general test
2023-10-16

Hoyeol Lee
Chairman
International TOSEL Committee

A certificate without the seal of the International TOSEL Committee is not valid as an official certificate, and the validity period of the certification is two years from the date of examination.

Actual Test 1

Section I

음원 QR 코드

Listening and Speaking

Part **A** ***Listen and Recognize***
5 Questions

Part **B** ***Listen and Respond***
5 Questions

Part **C** ***Listen and Retell***
15 Questions

Part **D** ***Listen and Speak***
5 Questions

PART A Listen and Recognize

Directions: You will hear English sentences. The sentences will be spoken TWICE. Listen carefully and choose the most suitable picture.

지시사항 1번에서 5번까지는 영어문장을 듣고, 들은 내용과 가장 관련 있는 그림을 고르는 문제입니다. 영어문장은 **두 번** 들려줍니다.

1.

(A)

(B)

(C)

(D)

2.

(A)

(B)

(C)

(D)

3.

(A)

(B)

(C)

(D)

4.

(A)

(B)

(C)

(D)

5.

(A)

(B)

(C)

(D)

PART B Listen and Respond

Directions: You will hear English sentences and answer choices (A), (B), (C), and (D). The sentences and the choices will be spoken TWICE. Listen carefully and choose the most suitable answer.

지시사항 6번부터 10번까지는 영어 문장을 듣고, 들은 말에 대한 가장 알맞은 대답을 고르는 문제입니다. 영어질문과 보기는 **두 번** 들려주며 (A), (B), (C), (D) 중에서 하나를 고르세요. B

6. Mark your answer on your answer sheet.

7. Mark your answer on your answer sheet.

8. Mark your answer on your answer sheet.

9. Mark your answer on your answer sheet.

10. Mark your answer on your answer sheet.

PART C Listen and Retell

Directions: You will hear short talks or conversations. They will be spoken TWICE. Listen carefully, read each question and choose the best answer.

지시사항 11번부터 25번까지는 짧은 대화나 이야기를 **두 번** 듣고, 주어진 질문에 가장 알맞은 답을 고르는 문제입니다. C

11. Who's on the phone?

(A)

(B)

(C)

(D)

12. What color are her flowers?

(A)

(B)

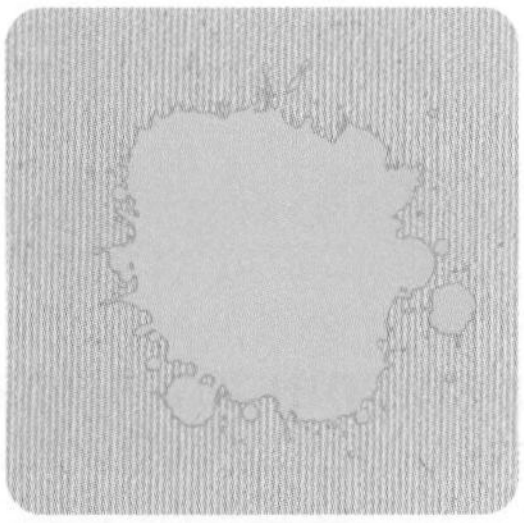
(C)

(D)

13. Where is his pencil?

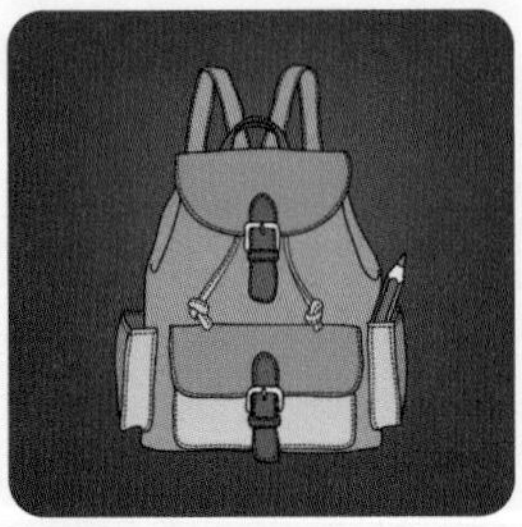
(A)

(B)

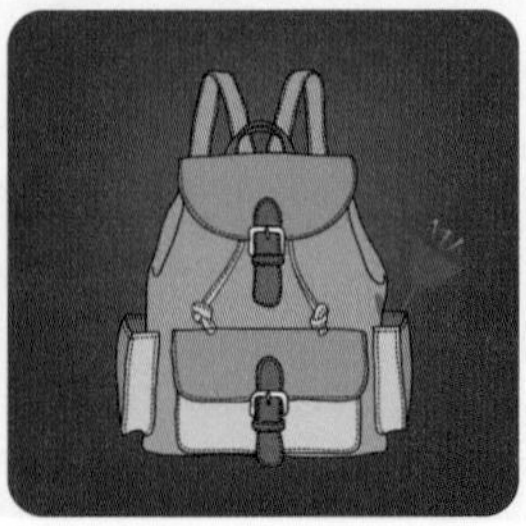
(C)

(D)

14. What can they do?

(A) ski
(B) swim
(C) sing
(D) dance

15. What is the weather like?

(A) windy
(B) hot
(C) cold
(D) rainy

16. Does the boy like pizza?

(A) Yes, he does.
(B) Sometimes.
(C) No, he doesn't.
(D) Never.

17. When is her English class?

(A) Friday
(B) Monday
(C) Tuesday
(D) Yesterday

[18-19]

18. What is John's favorite dessert?

(A) cake

(B) cookies

(C) apples

(D) chicken

19. What kind of cake does his mom make?

(A) vanilla

(B) chocolate

(C) carrot

(D) lemon

[20-21]

20. How does Craig finally wake up?

(A) His alarm clock rings.

(B) He falls out of the bed.

(C) His mother wakes him up.

(D) He has a bad dream.

21. What color are the numbers?

(A) red

(B) orange

(C) dark

(D) blue

[22-23]

22. What does the speaker do?

(A) watch TV

(B) study

(C) talk on the phone

(D) eat breakfast

23. Who does the dishes?

(A) her sister

(B) her mother

(C) nobody

(D) the speaker

[24-25]

24. Where do they see the elephants?

(A) at the zoo

(B) on a safari

(C) in a dream

(D) on the street

25. Who gets scared?

(A) the speaker

(B) the speaker's little sister

(C) the speaker's bigger sister

(D) the speaker's brother

PART D Listen and Speak

Directions: You will hear conversations in English. They will be spoken TWICE. After you listen to the conversations, read each question and choose the best response to what the last speaker says.

지시사항 26번부터 30번까지는 대화를 영어로 **두 번** 듣고, 대화의 마지막 질문이나 마지막 말 뒤에 이어질 가장 알맞은 응답을 주어진 질문에 맞게 고르는 문제입니다. D

26. What's next?

(A) It's red.

(B) It's old.

(C) It's new.

(D) It's broken.

27. What's next?

(A) Yes, it's next to the sink.

(B) No, the bathroom is dirty.

(C) Yes, there's a tower.

(D) No, it's in the bathroom.

28. What's next?

(A) I don't like to shop.

(B) I like the sports store.

(C) It's a good restaurant.

(D) There are many stores.

29. What's next?

(A) She's very nice.

(B) She's a doctor.

(C) She's my sister.

(D) She's very old.

30. What's next?

(A) Yes.

(B) Me, too!

(C) I can't.

(D) It can run.

Section II

Reading and Writing

Part **A** ***Sentence Completion***
5 Questions

Part **B** ***Situational Writing***
5 Questions

Part **C** ***Practical Reading and Retelling***
10 Questions

Part **D** ***General Reading and Retelling***
10 Questions

PART A Sentence Completion

Directions: You will see conversations with blanks. Read carefully and choose the one which best completes the blanks.

지시사항 1번에서 5번까지는 빈칸을 알맞게 채워 대화를 완성하는 문제입니다. 가장 알맞은 답을 고르세요.

1. A: How old are ______________?

B: I am 10 years old.

(A) you

(B) her

(C) she

(D) it

2. A: Where is the picture?

B: It's ______________ the wall.

(A) in

(B) on

(C) under

(D) with

3. A: Do you __________ lunch?

B: Yes, I'm hungry.

(A) want

(B) wants

(C) wanted

(D) wanting

4. A: __________ were you last night?

B: I was with Amy.

(A) Why

(B) Who

(C) When

(D) Where

5. A: Who is coming to the event?

B: Ellen __________ Alex will go there.

(A) or

(B) so

(C) but

(D) because

PART B Situational Writing

Directions: You will see pictures and incomplete sentences. Choose the one which best completes the sentences.

지시사항 6번부터 10번까지는 그림을 보고 문장을 완성하는 문제입니다. 가장 알맞은 답을 고르세요.

6.

Her skirt is ________________.

(A) green

(B) red

(C) yellow

(D) blue

7.

The man is ________________.

(A) cold

(B) young

(C) old

(D) hot

8.

Her dress is ________________.

(A) too big

(B) too short

(C) too small

(D) green

9.

They are ________________.

(A) resting

(B) sleeping

(C) eating

(D) dancing

10.

There is a turtle ________________ the pond.

(A) in

(B) behind

(C) above

(D) beside

PART C Practical Reading and Retelling

Directions: You will see practical reading materials. Each reading material is followed by questions about it. Choose the best answer to each question.

지시사항 11번부터 20번까지는 실용적 읽기자료에 관련된 문제입니다. 각 읽기자료 다음에는 질문이 제시됩니다. 각 질문에 해당하는 가장 알맞은 답을 고르세요.

For questions 11 – 12, refer to the following graph.

11. Which candy do the children like the most?

(A) hard candy

(B) soft candy

(C) chocolate

(D) gum

12. How many children were asked?

(A) 35

(B) 40

(C) 45

(D) 50

For questions 13 – 14, refer to the following graph.

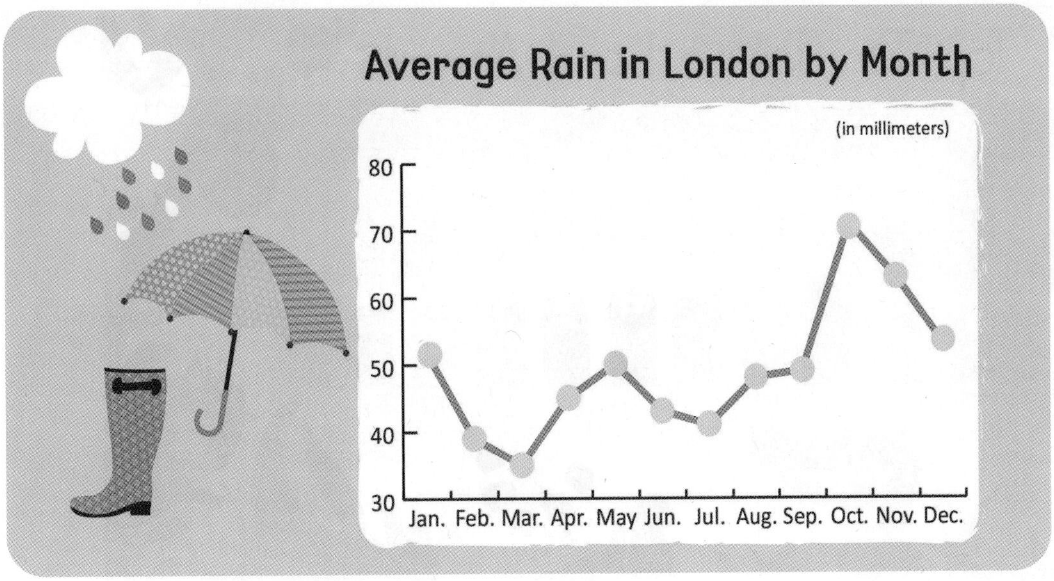

13. In which month does it rain the most?

(A) January

(B) May

(C) July

(D) October

14. Which month has less rain than April?

(A) January

(B) May

(C) July

(D) October

For questions 15 – 16, refer to the following graph.

15. Which of the following animals is the tallest?

(A) ostrich

(B) bear

(C) bison

(D) rhino

16. Which animals are the same size?

(A) elephant and giraffe

(B) buffalo and moose

(C) rhino and horse

(D) bison and bear

For questions 17 – 18, refer to the following chart.

Class Grades

Karen	Bill	Jordan	Stacy	Lauren
74%	63%	91%	74%	89%

17. Who has the worst grades in class?

(A) Karen

(B) Bill

(C) Jordan

(D) Lauren

18. Which two students have the same grades?

(A) Bill and Jordan

(B) Lauren and Jordan

(C) Karen and Stacy

(D) Bill and Lauren

For questions 19 – 20, refer to the following information.

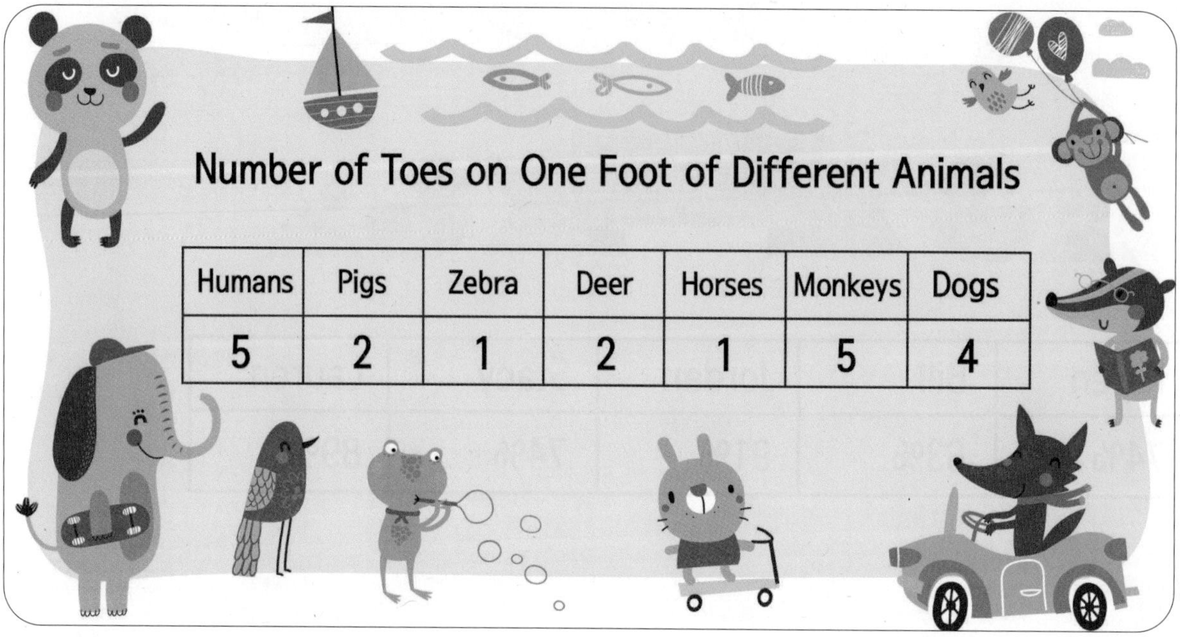

Number of Toes on One Foot of Different Animals

Humans	Pigs	Zebra	Deer	Horses	Monkeys	Dogs
5	2	1	2	1	5	4

19. Which animal has the most number of toes on one foot?

(A) monkey

(B) zebra

(C) pig

(D dog

20. In this list, in what place are humans for most number of toes?

(A) first

(B) second

(C) third

(D) fourth

PART D General Reading and Retelling

Directions: You will see various reading materials. Each reading material is followed by questions about it. Choose the best answer to each question.

지시사항 21번부터 30번까지는 다양한 읽기 자료에 관련된 문제입니다. 각 읽기 자료 다음에는 질문이 제시됩니다. 각 질문에 해당하는 가장 알맞은 답을 고르세요.

For questions 21 – 22, refer to the following passage.

Lions are big animals with sharp teeth. They eat smaller animals for food. They have strong legs and can run very fast. However, they also like to take long cat naps during most of the day. There are no lions in my country, but you can see them at the zoo.

21. What do lions eat?

(A) smaller animals

(B) fruit

(C) vegetables

(D) cake

22. Where can you see lions in the author's country?

(A) on the street

(B) at the supermarket

(C) at the zoo

(D) You cannot see them.

For questions 23 – 24, refer to the following passage.

May is a fun month in Korea. We have a special day just for children. It is called "Children's Day". We gets gifts and candy. We play games and eat our favorite foods. We do not even have to go to school! It is a great day to spend a fun time with our families.

23. Which month is fun in Korea?

(A) May

(B) June

(C) July

(D) August

24. Who is the special day for?

(A) mothers

(B) fathers

(C) teachers

(D) children

For questions 25 – 26, refer to the following passage.

August is very hot. I live by the ocean, so I love to go swimming. I also like to play in the sand. My sister and I make sand castles. Sometimes, we eat ice cream on the beach. I always get a little sad when summer ends and the weather gets colder.

25. Where does the author live?

(A) by the ocean

(B) by a lake

(C) in the sand

(D) in a castle

26. What does the author make with sister?

(A) tents

(B) sand castles

(C) ice cream

(D) ocean

For questions 27 – 28, refer to the following passage.

Sam likes his toy robot. It can walk and talk. He takes his robot to school with him. His friends think his robot is very fun. Sam and his friends play with it on the playground. Everyone takes turns sharing the robot, and they all have a fun time.

27. What can Sam's robot do?

(A) sing

(B) write

(C) walk and talk

(D) play and sing

28. Where do Sam and his friends play with his robot?

(A) at the station

(B) at home

(C) in the classroom

(D) on the playground

For questions 29 – 30, refer to the following passage.

Judy is making a paper doll. She wants to use glue. Judy looks inside her pencil case. She sees three pencils, two erasers, and a ruler. No glue! Judy looks inside her school bag. She does not see glue, but she finds some tape. She will just use that instead.

29. What is Judy making?

(A) glue

(B) paper

(C) a pencil case

(D) a paper doll

30. Where does Judy find the tape?

(A) on her pencil case

(B) in her pencil case

(C) in her school bag

(D) under her school bag

Actual Test 2

Section I

음원 QR 코드

Listening and Speaking

Part **A** ***Listen and Recognize***
5 Questions

Part **B** ***Listen and Respond***
5 Questions

Part **C** ***Listen and Retell***
15 Questions

Part **D** ***Listen and Speak***
5 Questions

PART A Listen and Recognize

Directions: You will hear English sentences. The sentences will be spoken TWICE. Listen carefully and choose the most suitable picture.

지시사항 1번에서 5번까지는 영어문장을 듣고, 들은 내용과 가장 관련 있는 그림을 고르는 문제입니다. 영어문장은 **두 번** 들려줍니다.

1.

(A)

(B)

(C)

(D)

2.

(A)

(B)

(C)

(D)

3.

(A)

(B)

(C)

(D)

4.

(A)

(B)

(C)

(D)

5.

(A)

(B)

(C)

(D)

PART B Listen and Respond

Directions: You will hear English sentences and answer choices (A), (B), (C), and (D). The sentences and the choices will be spoken TWICE. Listen carefully and choose the most suitable answer.

지시사항 6번부터 10번까지는 영어 문장을 듣고, 들은 말에 대한 가장 알맞은 대답을 고르는 문제입니다. 영어질문과 보기는 **두 번** 들려주며 (A), (B), (C), (D) 중에서 하나를 고르세요. B

6. Mark your answer on your answer sheet.

7. Mark your answer on your answer sheet.

8. Mark your answer on your answer sheet.

9. Mark your answer on your answer sheet.

10. Mark your answer on your answer sheet.

PART C Listen and Retell

Directions: You will hear short talks or conversations. They will be spoken TWICE. Listen carefully, read each question and choose the best answer.

지시사항 11번부터 25번까지는 짧은 대화나 이야기를 **두 번** 듣고, 주어진 질문에 가장 알맞은 답을 고르는 문제입니다. C

11. How will the teacher help?

(A)

(B)

(C)

(D)

12. Which picture shows the girl?

(A)

(B)

(C)

(D)

13. What is three dollars?

(A)

(B)

(C)

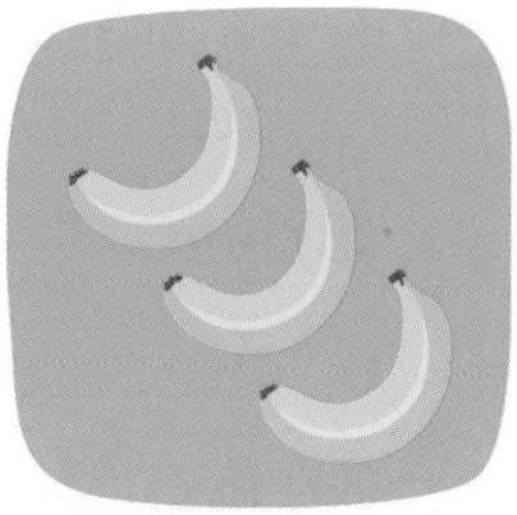

(D)

14. What's the girl's favorite ice cream?

(A) strawberry
(B) chocolate
(C) vanilla
(D) orange

15. What does the girl like to do?

(A) listen to songs
(B) sing songs
(C) play songs
(D) play video games

16. Where are they?

(A) in a park
(B) at school
(C) in a bedroom
(D) in a restaurant

17. How many sisters does the girl have?

(A) zero
(B) one
(C) two
(D) five

[18-19]

18. What does Joe love to do?

(A) take a bath

(B) blow bubbles

(C) feed the ducks

(D) talk with his mother

19. What is "Quack"?

(A) a bath tub

(B) a toy duck

(C) Joe's nickname

(D) a bubble machine

[20-21]

20. What does the boy like to throw for his dog?

(A) sticks

(B) balls

(C) pencils

(D) toys

21. What does the dog love to do?

(A) bite shoes

(B) eat sausages

(C) catch balls

(D) take a walk

[22-23]

22. What's the weather like?

(A) sunny

(B) windy

(C) snowy

(D) rainy

23. What will the girl NOT do?

(A) make snowmen

(B) have a snowball fight

(C) play with friends

(D) go to school

[24-25]

24. How big is a red panda?

(A) smaller than a dog

(B) bigger than a cat

(C) bigger than a tree

(D) smaller than a bamboo tree

25. What is NOT true about red pandas?

(A) They live in trees.

(B) You can find them in China.

(C) They eat a lot of bamboo.

(D) They do not have a tail.

PART D Listen and Speak

Directions: You will hear conversations in English. They will be spoken TWICE. After you listen to the conversations, read each question and choose the best response to what the last speaker says.

지시사항 26번부터 30번까지는 대화를 영어로 **두 번** 듣고, 대화의 마지막 질문이나 마지막 말 뒤에 이어질 가장 알맞은 응답을 주어진 질문에 맞게 고르는 문제입니다. D

26. What's next?

(A) I don't like pizza.

(B) Is there candy?

(C) It's not hot.

(D) Thanks, I'd love some.

27. What's next?

(A) They are very sweet.

(B) I like horses too!

(C) I lke hamburgers.

(D) They listen to music.

28. What's next?

(A) My name is James.

(B) His name is Mr. Jones.

(C) Her name is Ms. Jones.

(D) She's a teacher.

29. What's next?

(A) No, I don't like flowers.

(B) No, it isn't.

(C) Yes, it's an animal.

(D) Yes, I like animals.

30. What's next?

(A) Yes, you will.

(B) No, he isn't.

(C) OK, he is.

(D) Yes, you can.

Section II

Reading and Writing

Part A ***Sentence Completion***
5 Questions

Part B ***Situational Writing***
5 Questions

Part C ***Practical Reading and Retelling***
10 Questions

Part D ***General Reading and Retelling***
10 Questions

PART A Sentence Completion

Directions: You will see conversations with blanks. Read carefully and choose the one which best completes the blanks.

지시사항 1번에서 5번까지는 빈칸을 알맞게 채워 대화를 완성하는 문제입니다. 가장 알맞은 답을 고르세요.

1. A: ____________ is he?

B: He's in his classroom.

(A) Who
(B) What
(C) Where
(D) Why

2. A: What does your father ________?

B: He is a pilot.

(A) do
(B) did
(C) does
(D) doing

3. A: Can you help me ________ the car?

B: Sure. Pass the soap.

(A) wash
(B) washes
(C) washed
(D) washing

4. A: How old are ________ friends?

B: They are 11 years old.

(A) you
(B) your
(C) mine
(D) yours

5. A: What does she do ________ Mondays?

B: She goes to ballet class.

(A) in
(B) on
(C) at
(D) over

PART B Situational Writing

Directions: You will see pictures and incomplete sentences. Choose the one which best completes the sentences.

지시사항 6번부터 10번까지는 그림을 보고 문장을 완성하는 문제입니다. 가장 알맞은 답을 고르세요.

6.

The rabbit is ____________________.

(A) jumping
(B) sleeping
(C) eating
(D) playing

7.

My ____________________ is very old.

(A) uncle
(B) father
(C) grandfather
(D) grandmother

8.

The girl is putting cream on his _______.

(A) chin

(B) nose

(C) hand

(D) cheek

9.

The kids are ___________.

(A) in the park

(B) in the tree

(C) on the bench

(D) in the pond

10.

The woman is __________.

(A) feeding the dog

(B) talking to her friend

(C) short and blonde

(D) wearing glasses

PART C Practical Reading and Retelling

Directions: You will see practical reading materials. Each reading material is followed by questions about it. Choose the best answer to each question.

지시사항 11번부터 20번까지는 실용적 읽기자료에 관련된 문제입니다. 각 읽기자료 다음에는 질문이 제시됩니다. 각 질문에 해당하는 가장 알맞은 답을 고르세요.

For questions 11 – 12, refer to the following graph.

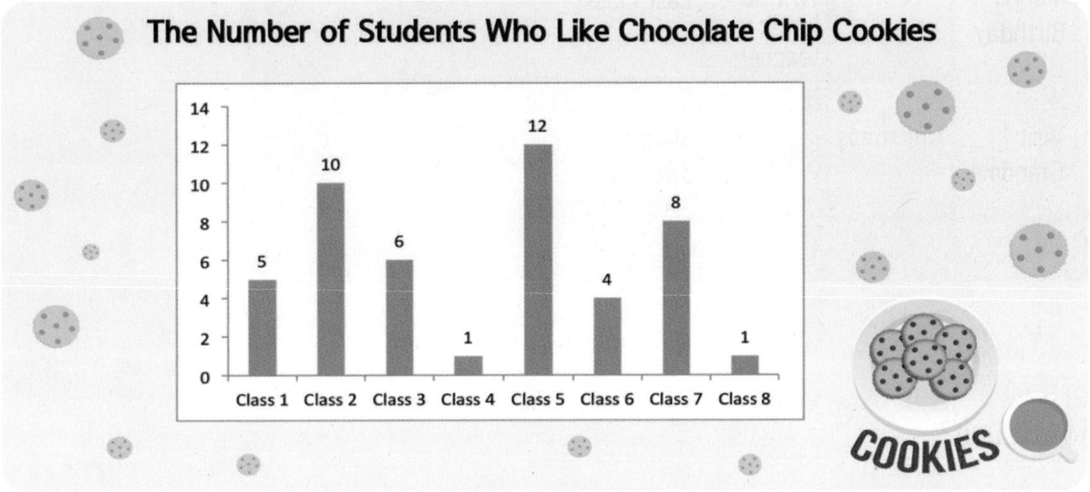

11. How many students in Class 3 like chocolate chip cookies?

(A) 4

(B) 6

(C) 10

(D) 12

12. Which class likes chocolate chip cookies the most?

(A) Class 1

(B) Class 3

(C) Class 5

(D) Class 7

For questions 13 – 14, refer to the following schedule.

Annie's Schedule

Sun	Mon	Tue	Wed	Thu	Fri	Sat
16	17 Mary's Birthday	18	19 Write a letter to teacher	20 Last class	21	22
23	24 Visit Grandma	25 Christmas	26	27 Shop for sweater	28	29

13. What month is it?

(A) January

(B) March

(C) August

(D) December

14. When does Annie visit grandma?

(A) on the 17th

(B) on the 19th

(C) on the 24th

(D) on the 27th

For questions 15 – 16, refer to the following picture.

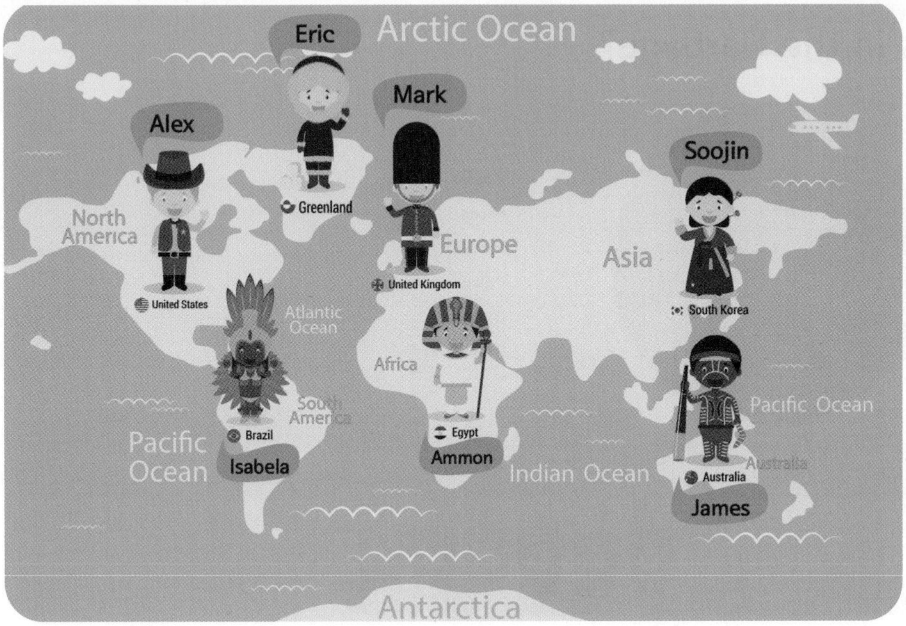

15. Where does Alex live?

(A) in Korea

(B) in America

(C) in England

(D) in Africa

16. Who lives in Asia?

(A) Eric

(B) Soojin

(C) Isabela

(D) Mark

For questions 17 – 18, refer to the following chart.

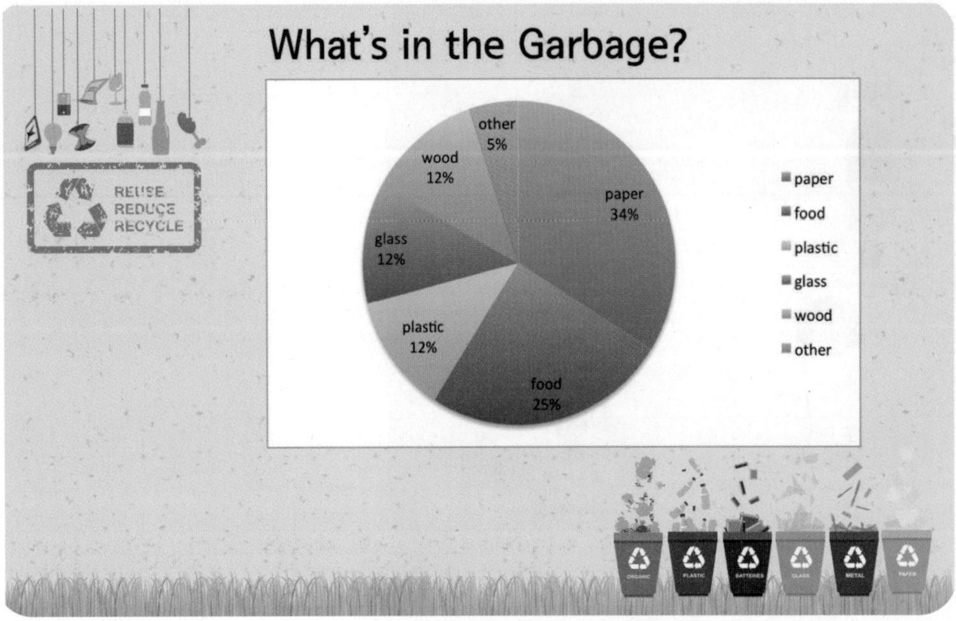

17. What makes the most garbage?

(A) food

(B) plastic

(C) paper

(D) glass

18. Which three are the same percentage?

(A) food, plastic, and glass

(B) plastic, glass, and wood

(C) glass, wood, and other

(D) food, paper, and other

For questions 19 – 20, refer to the following picture.

19. Where is the clock?

(A) in the bedroom

(B) in the kitchen

(C) in the living room

(D) in the study room

20. Where is the bedroom?

(A) on the balcony

(B) between the bathroom and the study room

(C) next to the living room

(D) between the living room and the kitchen

PART D General Reading and Retelling

Directions: You will see various reading materials. Each reading material is followed by questions about it. Choose the best answer to each question.

지시사항 21번부터 30번까지는 다양한 읽기 자료에 관련된 문제입니다. 각 읽기 자료 다음에는 질문이 제시됩니다. 각 질문에 해당하는 가장 알맞은 답을 고르세요.

For questions 21 – 22, refer to the following passage.

Skiing is one of my favorite winter sports. Every winter, I go with my father and climb up the snowy hills. We do not ski very fast, but it is still fun. Even if I fall, it does not hurt because the snow is so soft.

21. What does the writer like to do in the winter?

(A) make snowmen

(B) play chess

(C) run on mountains

(D) ski on hills

22. According to the passage, which sentence is true?

(A) They ski on tall mountains.

(B) The writer skis alone.

(C) It does not hurt when the writer falls.

(D) The writer does not have fun when they skis.

For questions 23 – 24, refer to the following passage.

My friend Lisa has the perfect hobby. She collects buttons. She has over one hundred different buttons. She finds buttons everywhere. She finds them in the park, under sofas, and even at school. Sometimes she buys them at the sewing shop. She loves all buttons, but her favorite ones are purple.

23. How many buttons does Lisa have?

(A) less than ten
(B) just fifty
(C) over one hundred
(D) over one thousand

24. What color are her favorites?

(A) white
(B) purple
(C) green
(D) red

For questions 25 – 26, refer to the following passage.

My dad loves to shop at many different stores, but his favorite is the sports store. He spends a lot of time and money there. For my birthday, my dad took me to the sports store and bought me a basketball. We went back home and played for 3 hours! I was tired but had a lot of fun.

25. What kind of store does the dad like the most?

(A) grocery store

(B) clothes store

(C) shoes store

(D) sports store

26. What did the writer get for his birthday?

(A) a basketball

(B) a baseball

(C) a tennis ball

(D) a soccer ball

For questions 27 – 28, refer to the following passage.

Mice are small animals. Most are gray or brown. They live in the grass and sometimes in the walls of people's homes. People are scared of mice, but they are not usually dangerous. Many people think mice like cheese, but they actually like sweet food more. It is easier to catch a mouse with sweets than with cheese.

27. What color are most mice?

(A) black only
(B) gray only
(C) gray or brown
(D) brown and black

28. What do mice like to do?

(A) hurt and scare people
(B) swim in the water
(C) play with small animals
(D) eat sweet food

For questions 29 – 30, refer to the following passage.

Tom is a good baseball player. He is very strong and can hit the ball a long way. This year he hit 10 homeruns! He runs fast and is good at catching the ball. He is always kind to other players as well. This year he was chosen as the team MVP.

29. What does Tom NOT do?

(A) kick the ball

(B) catch the ball

(C) hit the ball

(D) run very fast

30. What kind of player is Tom?

(A) a slow runner

(B) a bad catcher

(C) a good hitter

(D) a good dancer

Actual Test 3

Section I

음원 QR 코드

Listening and Speaking

Part **A** ***Listen and Recognize***
5 Questions

Part **B** ***Listen and Respond***
5 Questions

Part **C** ***Listen and Retell***
15 Questions

Part **D** ***Listen and Speak***
5 Questions

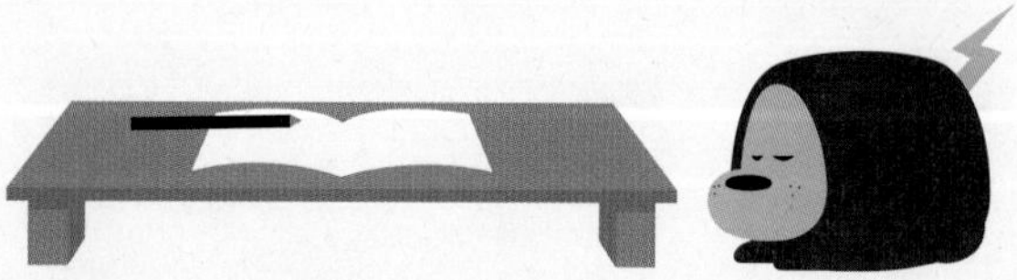

PART A Listen and Recognize

Directions: You will hear English sentences. The sentences will be spoken TWICE. Listen carefully and choose the most suitable picture.

지시사항 1번에서 5번까지는 영어문장을 듣고, 들은 내용과 가장 관련 있는 그림을 고르는 문제입니다. 영어문장은 **두 번** 들려줍니다.

1.

(A)

(B)

(C)

(D)

2.

(A)

(B)

(C)

(D)

3.

(A)

(B)

(C)

(D)

4.

(A)

(B)

(C)

(D)

5.

(A)

(B)

(C)

(D)

PART B Listen and Respond

Directions: You will hear English sentences and answer choices (A), (B), (C), and (D). The sentences and the choices will be spoken TWICE. Listen carefully and choose the most suitable answer.

지시사항 6번부터 10번까지는 영어 문장을 듣고, 들은 말에 대한 가장 알맞은 대답을 고르는 문제입니다. 영어질문과 보기는 **두 번** 들려주며 (A), (B), (C), (D) 중에서 하나를 고르세요. B

6. Mark your answer on your answer sheet.

7. Mark your answer on your answer sheet.

8. Mark your answer on your answer sheet.

9. Mark your answer on your answer sheet.

10. Mark your answer on your answer sheet.

PART C Listen and Retell

Directions: You will hear short talks or conversations. They will be spoken TWICE. Listen carefully, read each question and choose the best answer.

지시사항 11번부터 25번까지는 짧은 대화나 이야기를 **두 번** 듣고, 주어진 질문에 가장 알맞은 답을 고르는 문제입니다. C

11. Where is the flower shop?

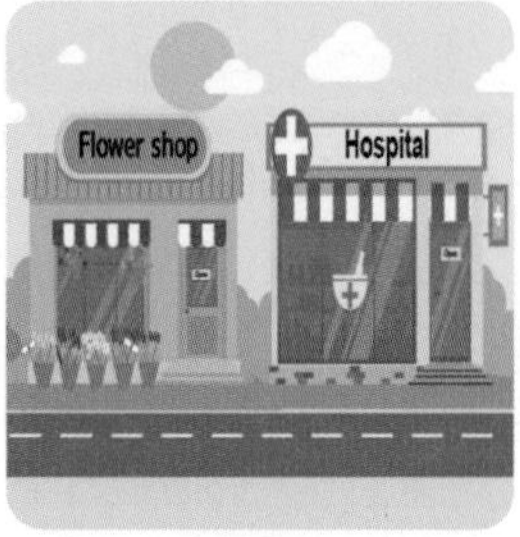

(A)

(B)

(C)

(D)

12. What does the girl want to have?

(A)

(B)

(C)

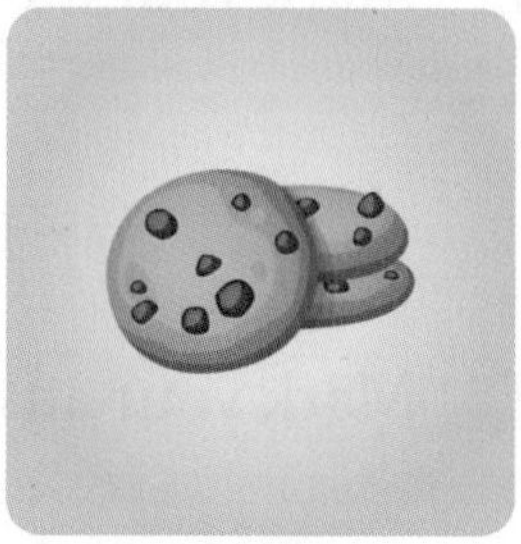
(D)

13. What are they doing after school?

(A)

(B)

(C)

(D)

14. Why is his brother happy?

(A) He studies hard.
(B) He plays soccer.
(C) He watches TV.
(D) He reads books.

15. What does the girl's mom probably do?

(A) She's a teacher.
(B) She's a pilot.
(C) She's a nurse.
(D) She's a firefighter.

16. What does the boy like?

(A) music
(B) movies
(C) soccer
(D) books

17. How is the weather?

(A) It's windy.
(B) It's cloudy.
(C) It's too hot.
(D) It's raining.

[18-19]

18. What did the mom do?

(A) She gave the cat food.

(B) She put the cat outside.

(C) She put the cat to bed.

(D) She washed the cat.

19. What did the cat do after eating?

(A) play

(B) walk

(C) sleep

(D) eat

[20-21]

20. Who does Sally go to the library with?

(A) her mother

(B) her brother

(C) her father

(D) her sister

21. When does Sally watch cartoons?

(A) Monday and Tuesday

(B) Sunday and Monday

(C) Saturday and Sunday

(D) Friday and Saturday

[22-23]

22. What does his sister do?

(A) She's a teacher.

(B) She's a pilot.

(C) She's a doctor.

(D) She's a student.

23. What does she do on the weekends?

(A) study English

(B) study Chinese

(C) take a test

(D) travel to China

[24-25]

24. How old will Julie be?

(A) eight years old

(B) nine years old

(C) ten years old

(D) eleven years old

25. Where is she going on her birthday?

(A) to the zoo

(B) to the library

(C) to the park

(D) to the swimming pool

PART D Listen and Speak

Directions: You will hear conversations in English. They will be spoken TWICE. After you listen to the conversations, read each question and choose the best response to what the last speaker says.

지시사항 26번부터 30번까지는 대화를 영어로 **두 번** 듣고, 대화의 마지막 질문이나 마지막 말 뒤에 이어질 가장 알맞은 응답을 주어진 질문에 맞게 고르는 문제입니다. D

26. What's next?

(A) A sandwich.

(B) A ball.

(C) An eraser.

(D) A pot.

27. What's next?

(A) It's green.

(B) Really?

(C) It's old.

(D) Where is your mom?

28. What's next?

(A) No, thanks.

(B) Yes, please.

(C) Yes, it is.

(D) No, he isn't.

29. What's next?

(A) I have a headache.

(B) I have a hat.

(C) I have a drink.

(D) I have a book.

30. What's next?

(A) Are you sure?

(B) Who is he?

(C) Where is the bank?

(D) No, I don't have any money.

Section II

Reading and Writing

Part **A** ***Sentence Completion***
5 Questions

Part **B** ***Situational Writing***
5 Questions

Part **C** ***Practical Reading and Retelling***
10 Questions

Part **D** ***General Reading and Retelling***
10 Questions

PART A Sentence Completion

Directions: You will see conversations with blanks. Read carefully and choose the one which best completes the blanks.

지시사항 1번에서 5번까지는 빈칸을 알맞게 채워 대화를 완성하는 문제입니다. 가장 알맞은 답을 고르세요.

1. A: How ________ are you?
B: I'm nine years old.

(A) many
(B) much
(C) old
(D) time

2. A: Where do you ________?
B: In Seoul, Korea.

(A) live
(B) living
(C) to live
(D) are living

3. A: ________ do you do on Saturdays?
B: I go to my grandmother's house.

(A) What
(B) When
(C) Why
(D) How

4. A: Did you see the movie?
B: Yes, but I don't want to spoil the movie ________ you see it.

(A) after
(B) when
(C) before
(D) because

5. A: How was the weather yesterday?
B: It was the ________!

(A) hot
(B) hotter
(C) hottest
(D) most hot

PART B Situational Writing

Directions: You will see pictures and incomplete sentences. Choose the one which best completes the sentences.

지시사항 6번부터 10번까지는 그림을 보고 문장을 완성하는 문제입니다. 가장 알맞은 답을 고르세요.

6.

I like going to __________________.

(A) school

(B) the park

(C) the library

(D) the swimming pool

7.

There is a picture __________ the lamps.

(A) across

(B) into

(C) between

(D) in front of

8.

This is my __________________ Jane.

(A) older sister

(B) baby sister

(C) big brother

(D) older brother

9.

They are __________________.

(A) watching TV

(B) eating breakfast

(C) talking to their parents

(D) doing their homework

10.

My father __________________ than my mother.

(A) is cute

(B) is taller

(C) is fastest

(D) was short

PART C Practical Reading and Retelling

Directions: You will see practical reading materials. Each reading material is followed by questions about it. Choose the best answer to each question.

지시사항 11번부터 20번까지는 실용적 읽기자료에 관련된 문제입니다. 각 읽기자료 다음에는 질문이 제시됩니다. 각 질문에 해당하는 가장 알맞은 답을 고르세요.

For questions 11 – 12, refer to the following schedule.

Peter's Weekly Schedule

Sun	Mon	Tues	Weds
Go to Grandmother's House	Go to the library	Play soccer	Play computer games
Thurs	**Fri**	**Sat**	Memo
Fly a kite in the park	Stay at home	Help Mom with the shop	

11. What does Peter do on Mondays?

(A) stay at home

(B) go to the library

(C) help Mom with the shop

(D) go to the Grandmother's house

12. What does Peter NOT have on his schedule?

(A) play soccer

(B) ride a bike

(C) fly a kite in the park

(D) play computer games

For questions 13 – 14, refer to the following graph.

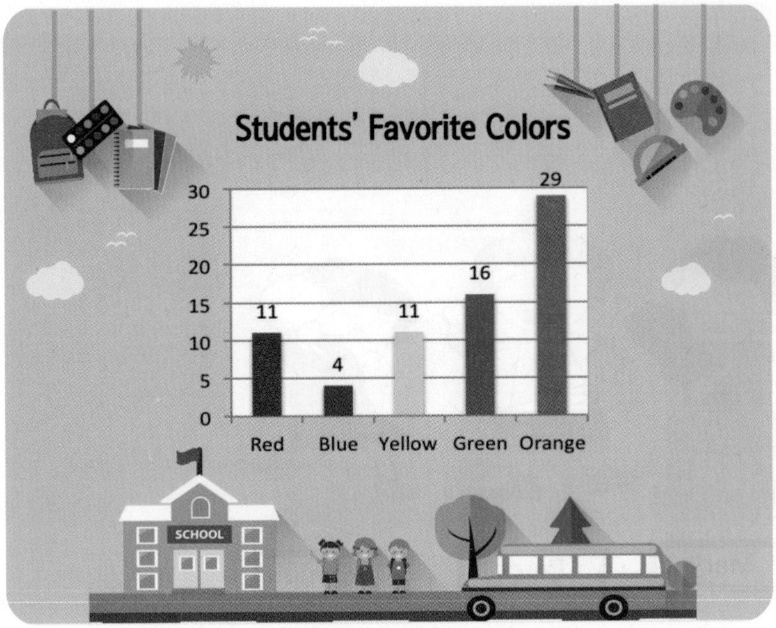

13. How many students like red?

(A) 4

(B) 11

(C) 17

(D) 29

14. What color do the students like the least?

(A) red

(B) orange

(C) green

(D) blue

For questions 15 – 16, refer to the following information.

15. What are they doing?

(A) playing soccer

(B) studying English

(C) making speeches

(D) playing musical instruments

16. Who is wearing a blue T-shirt?

(A) Sam

(B) Peter

(C) Annie

(D) Sophie

For questions 17 – 18, refer to the following information.

Using a Bus in Britain

1. Always get on the bus using the front door.
2. Pay the driver when you get on the bus.
3. Take a seat.
4. Press the bell when you want the bus to stop.
5. Leave the bus using the middle doors of the bus.

17. Where do British people get on the bus?

(A) at the front door

(B) at the middle door

(C) at the back door

(D) at any door

18. What do British people do to get off the bus?

(A) stand up

(B) press the bell

(C) say 'Excuse me?'

(D) talk to the driver

For questions 19 – 20, refer to the following information.

19. What day is the school fair?

(A) Friday

(B) Saturday

(C) Sunday

(D) Monday

20. What can you NOT do at the fair?

(A) play games

(B) win fish

(C) play basketball

(D) eat some homemade food

PART D General Reading and Retelling

Directions: You will see various reading materials. Each reading material is followed by questions about it. Choose the best answer to each question.

지시사항 21번부터 30번까지는 다양한 읽기 자료에 관련된 문제입니다. 각 읽기 자료 다음에는 질문이 제시됩니다. 각 질문에 해당하는 가장 알맞은 답을 고르세요.

For questions 21 – 22, refer to the following passage.

It is my birthday today. I am ten years old. There will be a party at my house today at 1 o'clock. My friends are coming to my house to play! My mom is making pizza and lemonade. We will also eat cake and ice cream! After eating, we will sing and dance all day.

21. What will Mom make for the party?

(A) pizza
(B) cake
(C) ice cream
(D) sandwiches

22. Where is the party?

(A) the park
(B) a restaurant
(C) his school
(D) his house

For questions 23 – 24, refer to the following passage.

London is the biggest city in England. There is a famous clock called Big Ben. You can see it in many pictures and movies. London also has the River Thames that goes through the city. People can take boat trips on the river and take photos of famous buildings.

23. What is Big Ben?

(A) a clock

(B) a river

(C) a boat

(D) a city

24. What can you do on the River Thames?

(A) have a picnic

(B) take your coat

(C) take a boat trip

(D) make a building

For questions 25 – 26, refer to the following passage.

Valentine's Day is celebrated in many countries. Valentine's Day is on February 14th every year. In America and Canada, boys and girls give each other Valentine's Day cards and flowers and go to dinner. In Asia, girls give boys chocolates and other gifts. The boys then give girls gifts on White Day, which is on March 14th.

25. When is Valentine's Day?

(A) after White Day
(B) March
(C) February
(D) every month

26. What happens on White Day in Asia?

(A) There are no gifts.
(B) Girls give boys gifts.
(C) Boys give girls gifts.
(D) They give gifts to each other.

For questions 27 – 28, refer to the following passage.

Sam has a sister. Her name is Donna. Sam and Donna play together every day. Donna likes to sing and play soccer. Sam likes to play baseball and go swimming. Sam and Donna always go to the park together. They play for many hours and always go back home late.

27. Who likes soccer?

(A) Sam
(B) Donna
(C) both of them
(D) neither of them

28. How often do they play?

(A) always
(B) never
(C) rarely
(D) sometimes

For questions 29 – 30, refer to the following passage.

James has a busy day today. He has to go to school and study English, history, and math. Afterwards, James will take the bus to town and go to the library. He has to return his library books. He will then go to the store, and his mother will buy him a hat.

29. Where does James NOT have to go today?

(A) school

(B) the store

(C) the library

(D) the train station

30. What will his mother buy him?

(A) a bag

(B) a hat

(C) a bus

(D) a book

Actual Test 4

Section I

음원 QR 코드

Listening and Speaking

Part **A** ***Listen and Recognize***
5 Questions

Part **B** ***Listen and Respond***
5 Questions

Part **C** ***Listen and Retell***
15 Questions

Part **D** ***Listen and Speak***
5 Questions

PART A Listen and Recognize

Directions: You will hear English sentences. The sentences will be spoken TWICE. Listen carefully and choose the most suitable picture.

지시사항 1번에서 5번까지는 영어문장을 듣고, 들은 내용과 가장 관련 있는 그림을 고르는 문제입니다. 영어문장은 **두 번** 들려줍니다.

1.

(A)

(B)

(C)

(D)

2.

(A)

(B)

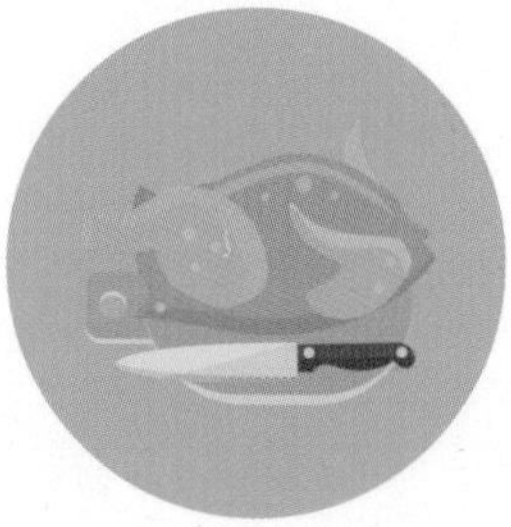

(C)

(D)

3.

(A)

(B)

(C)

(D)

4.

(A)

(B)

(C)

(D)

5.

(A)

(B)

(C)

(D)

PART B Listen and Respond

Directions: You will hear English sentences and answer choices (A), (B), (C), and (D). The sentences and the choices will be spoken TWICE. Listen carefully and choose the most suitable answer.

지시사항 6번부터 10번까지는 영어 문장을 듣고, 들은 말에 대한 가장 알맞은 대답을 고르는 문제입니다. 영어질문과 보기는 **두 번** 들려주며 (A), (B), (C), (D) 중에서 하나를 고르세요.

6. Mark your answer on your answer sheet.

7. Mark your answer on your answer sheet.

8. Mark your answer on your answer sheet.

9. Mark your answer on your answer sheet.

10. Mark your answer on your answer sheet.

PART C Listen and Retell

Directions: You will hear short talks or conversations. They will be spoken TWICE. Listen carefully, read each question and choose the best answer.

지시사항 11번부터 25번까지는 짧은 대화나 이야기를 **두 번** 듣고, 주어진 질문에 가장 알맞은 답을 고르는 문제입니다.

11. Where is Brenda?

(A)

(B)

(C)

(D)

12. What does the girl want?

(A)

(B)

(C)

(D)

13. Who is the boy's father?

(A)

(B)

(C)

(D)

14. Where is the boy's cup?

(A) It's on the floor.
(B) It's on the table.
(C) It's in the cupboard.
(D) It's in the sink.

15. What's wrong with the girl?

(A) She has a headache.
(B) She has a stomachache.
(C) Her leg hurts.
(D) Her neck hurts.

16. Where are they?

(A) at a playground
(B) at a store
(C) in a classroom
(D) in a car

17. What does the boy like?

(A) the red sweater
(B) the blue sweater
(C) the red shirt
(D) the blue shirt

[18-19]

18. When does the boy eat a snack at school?

(A) at 10:00 AM
(B) at 10:30 AM
(C) at 11:00 AM
(D) at 11:30 AM

19. What can the boy NOT eat at school?

(A) vegetables
(B) cheese
(C) potato chips
(D) fruit

[20-21]

20. How much did each student pay?

(A) $3.00
(B) $6.00
(C) $9.00
(D) $10.00

21. What will the school do with the ticket money?

(A) build more classrooms
(B) build a new playground
(C) have more parties
(D) buy more computers

[22-23]

22. What does the boy want to be?

(A) an author

(B) an actor

(C) a musician

(D) a teacher

23. Why are the boy's parents excited?

(A) The boy will be in a play.

(B) The boy will get good grades.

(C) They will see a movie.

(D) They will go to an acting school.

[24-25]

24. How many hours of sunshine does Yellowknife have in December?

(A) four hours every day

(B) five hours every day

(C) nine hours every day

(D) fifteen hours every day

25. What clothing does the girl NOT talk about?

(A) boots

(B) hat

(C) scarf

(D) mittens

PART D Listen and Speak

Directions: You will hear conversations in English. They will be spoken TWICE. After you listen to the conversations, read each question and choose the best response to what the last speaker says.

지시사항 26번부터 30번까지는 대화를 영어로 **두 번** 듣고, 대화의 마지막 질문이나 마지막 말 뒤에 이어질 가장 알맞은 응답을 주어진 질문에 맞게 고르는 문제입니다. D

26. What's next?

(A) I need a bath.

(B) That looks great.

(C) Oh no, that's too bad.

(D) I have black socks.

27. What's next?

(A) They're in my garden.

(B) I have a lot of homework.

(C) You missed the bus.

(D) They're for my mother.

28. What's next?

(A) Yes, of course.

(B) Sure, see you later.

(C) Yes, you can lose them.

(D) I didn't know that.

29. What's next?

(A) They're interesting.

(B) It's a little boring.

(C) It's the best song.

(D) They sell books.

30. What's next?

(A) No, I don't know you.

(B) I'm free every day.

(C) No, I don't. Sorry.

(D) It's three-thirty.

Section II

Reading and Writing

Part **A** ***Sentence Completion***
5 Questions

Part **B** ***Situational Writing***
5 Questions

Part **C** ***Practical Reading and Retelling***
10 Questions

Part **D** ***General Reading and Retelling***
10 Questions

PART A Sentence Completion

Directions: You will see conversations with blanks. Read carefully and choose the one which best completes the blanks.

지시사항 1번에서 5번까지는 빈칸을 알맞게 채워 대화를 완성하는 문제입니다. 가장 알맞은 답을 고르세요.

1. A: What is Dad doing in the kitchen?

B: He's ________ the dishes.

(A) do

(B) does

(C) doing

(D) doed

2. A: ______________ is the name of your dog?

B: It's Matilda.

(A) Who

(B) What

(C) When

(D) Where

3. A: Come join the baseball team.

B: Sorry, I'm not very good ________ sports.

(A) at

(B) by

(C) to

(D) of

4. A: Can we walk to John's house?

B: No, it's too far ________.

(A) walk

(B) to walk

(C) walking

(D) will walk

5. A: ________ you turn on the fan? I'm hot.

B: Really? Not me. I feel cold.

(A) Do

(B) Can

(C) Does

(D) Should

PART B Situational Writing

Directions: You will see pictures and incomplete sentences. Choose the one which best completes the sentences.

지시사항 6번부터 10번까지는 그림을 보고 문장을 완성하는 문제입니다. 가장 알맞은 답을 고르세요.

6.

The woman is ________.

(A) setting a table

(B) playing the piano

(C) painting a picture

(D) listening to music

7.

The children are ____________________ the rollercoaster.

(A) waiting in line for

(B) getting on

(C) getting off

(D) riding

8. 

The family is ________________.

(A) throwing snowballs

(B) building a snowman

(C) sliding down a snowy hill

(D) clearing snow off the road

9. 

The girl is wearing _______.

(A) white mittens

(B) blue pants

(C) a green hat

(D) a pink coat

10. 

The woman is ________________.

(A) reading a magazine

(B) reading a newspaper

(C) talking on a phone

(D) talking to a nurse

PART C Practical Reading and Retelling

Directions: You will see practical reading materials. Each reading material is followed by questions about it. Choose the best answer to each question.

지시사항 11번부터 20번까지는 실용적 읽기자료에 관련된 문제입니다. 각 읽기자료 다음에는 질문이 제시됩니다. 각 질문에 해당하는 가장 알맞은 답을 고르세요.

For questions 11 – 12, refer to the following information.

Thornhill Guitar Lessons for Kids

Class	Place	Day	Time	Start Date
Level 1	St. Jean Elementary	Sunday	3:00 PM – 4:30 PM	Sept. 26
Level 2	Bayview High School	Monday	5:30 PM – 6:30 PM	Sept. 27
Level 3	Woods Elementary	Thursday	6:00 PM – 7:00 PM	Sept. 30
Level 4	Thornela High School	Saturday	9:00 PM – 10:00 PM	Oct. 2

11. What starts on Sept. 30?

(A) Level 1

(B) Level 2

(C) Level 3

(D) Level 4

12. Where are Saturday lessons offered?

(A) at St. Jean Elementary

(B) at Bayview High School

(C) at Woods Elementary

(D) at Thornela High School

For questions 13 – 14, refer to the following information.

13. When is it cheapest to bowl?

(A) Monday - Friday daytime

(B) Monday - Thursday evening

(C) Friday - Saturday evening

(D) all day Sunday

14. How much does one game cost on a Friday night?

(A) $3.00

(B) $3.50

(C) $4.50

(D) $5.50

For questions 15 – 16, refer to the following information.

15. What subject do tutors NOT teach?

(A) English
(B) history
(C) math
(D) science

16. How much is a two-hour lesson?

(A) $25.00
(B) $35.00
(C) $60.00
(D) $70.00

For questions 17 – 18, refer to the following information.

17. What do visitors do first?

(A) eat dinner

(B) look at the stars

(C) look at animals at night

(D) look at animals in the day

18. What kind of animals do visitors see?

(A) snakes

(B) camels

(C) black bears

(D) koalas

For questions 19 – 20, refer to the following information.

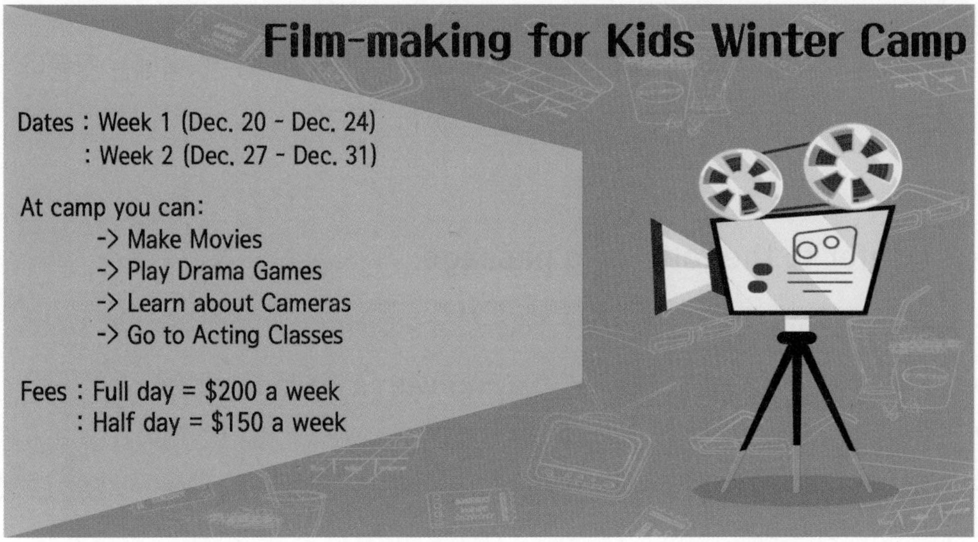

19. What will students NOT learn at the camp?

(A) how to act

(B) how to draw

(C) how to take pictures

(D) how to make movies

20. How much is one week at the half-day camp?

(A) $150.00

(B) $200.00

(C) $300.00

(D) $400.00

PART D General Reading and Retelling

Directions: You will see various reading materials. Each reading material is followed by questions about it. Choose the best answer to each question.

지시사항 21번부터 30번까지는 다양한 읽기 자료에 관련된 문제입니다. 각 읽기 자료 다음에는 질문이 제시됩니다. 각 질문에 해당하는 가장 알맞은 답을 고르세요.

For questions 21 – 22, refer to the following passage.

Last night I had an interesting dream. I was playing with a balloon in my yard. Suddenly, I started to fly up into the air like a bird. I went up to the clouds. I looked down and saw the mountains. I saw the park and the river. I was not afraid. Then I woke up.

21. What did the writer see in her dream?

(A) a lake

(B) a park

(C) a library

(D) a playground

22. How did the writer feel in her dream?

(A) sad

(B) afraid

(C) worried

(D) interested

For questions 23 – 24, refer to the following passage.

My name is Simon, and I am from England. However, these days I live in India. We move often because of my father's job. Last year we lived in Indonesia. Two years ago, we lived in China. Next year we will move to Thailand. Every year I change schools. It is not easy, because I have to make new friends each time.

23. Where does the boy live now?

(A) in India
(B) in China
(C) in England
(D) in Thailand

24. What is difficult for the boy?

(A) changing houses
(B) doing school work
(C) making new friends
(D) learning new languages

For questions 25 – 26, refer to the following passage.

Bark spiders live in Madagascar. They make the largest spider webs in the world. Their webs can be over 25 meters long. Only bark spiders build their webs over rivers. Their webs catch flying insects. Bark spiders mainly eat flies and mosquitoes.

25. Where do bark spiders build their webs?

(A) over rivers

(B) on the ground

(C) in thick forests

(D) inside buildings

26. What do bark spiders mainly eat?

(A) their webs

(B) other spiders

(C) Madagascar

(D) flies and mosquitoes

For questions 27 – 28, refer to the following passage.

Jordan Romero was very young, but he decided to climb seven of the tallest mountains in the world. At 9 years old, Jordan climbed Mount Kilimanjaro in Tanzania. In 2010, he became the youngest person to climb the tallest mountain in the world - Mount Everest. He was just 13 years old.

27. How old was Jordan when he climbed Mount Kilimanjaro?

(A) 5 years old
(B) 7 years old
(C) 9 years old
(D) 13 years old

28. What is special about Jordan?

(A) He was the first to climb Mount Everest.
(B) He was the youngest to climb Mount Everest.
(C) He was the youngest to climb Mount Kilimanjaro.
(D) He was the first to climb seven of the tallest mountains

For questions 29 – 30, refer to the following passage.

Our school has a garden. My classmates and I work in the garden every day. We water the plants and keep them healthy. There are vegetables and herbs in our garden. Our school cafeteria uses the food to make delicious lunches. We enjoy eating our fresh vegetables.

29. Where is the garden?

(A) at a teacher's home

(B) at the students' school

(C) in the country

(D) in a garden center

30. What does the school do with the vegetables?

(A) use them to make lunches for kids

(B) give them to poor people

(C) sell them to the students' parents

(D) sell them at a farmers' market

Actual Test 5

Section I

음원 QR 코드

Listening and Speaking

Part **A** ***Listen and Recognize***
5 Questions

Part **B** ***Listen and Respond***
5 Questions

Part **C** ***Listen and Retell***
15 Questions

Part **D** ***Listen and Speak***
5 Questions

PART A Listen and Recognize

Directions: You will hear English sentences. The sentences will be spoken TWICE. Listen carefully and choose the most suitable picture.

지시사항 1번에서 5번까지는 영어문장을 듣고, 들은 내용과 가장 관련 있는 그림을 고르는 문제입니다. 영어문장은 **두 번** 들려줍니다. (A)

1.

(A)

(B)

(C)

(D)

2.

(A)

(B)

(C)

(D)

3.

(A)

(B)

(C)

(D)

4.

(A)

(B)

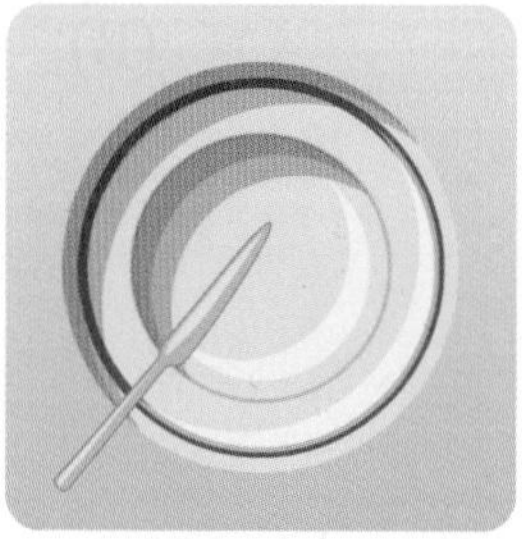
(C)

(D)

5.

(A)

(B)

(C)

(D)

PART B Listen and Respond

Directions: You will hear English sentences and answer choices (A), (B), (C), and (D). The sentences and the choices will be spoken TWICE. Listen carefully and choose the most suitable answer.

지시사항 6번부터 10번까지는 영어 문장을 듣고, 들은 말에 대한 가장 알맞은 대답을 고르는 문제입니다. 영어질문과 보기는 **두 번** 들려주며 (A), (B), (C), (D) 중에서 하나를 고르세요. B

6. Mark your answer on your answer sheet.

7. Mark your answer on your answer sheet.

8. Mark your answer on your answer sheet.

9. Mark your answer on your answer sheet.

10. Mark your answer on your answer sheet.

PART C Listen and Retell

Directions: You will hear short talks or conversations. They will be spoken TWICE. Listen carefully, read each question and choose the best answer.

지시사항 11번부터 25번까지는 짧은 대화나 이야기를 **두 번** 듣고, 주어진 질문에 가장 알맞은 답을 고르는 문제입니다. C

11. Where are they?

(A) (B) (C) (D)

12. Who fell into the pool?

(A) (B) (C) (D)

13. When is the basketball game?

(A) (B) (C) (D)

14. What was the boy doing?

(A) lying
(B) sleeping
(C) laughing
(D) studying

15. What is the girl's brother doing?

(A) playing at the playground
(B) playing the piano at home
(C) practicing the flute at home
(D) taking a piano lesson at school

16. How will they get to the library?

(A) by subway
(B) by bike
(C) by bus
(D) by car

17. Why will the girl NOT play computer games?

(A) She has to do homework.
(B) She has to clean her room.
(C) She has to help her parents.
(D) She has to go to class.

[18-19]

18. Who gave the girl a camera?

(A) her parents
(B) her grandparents
(C) her aunt
(D) her uncle

19. What did the girl take pictures of last?

(A) a tree
(B) a duck
(C) some people
(D) some flowers

[20-21]

20. What kind of pizza do the boys eat?

(A) ham and pineapple
(B) potato and pineapple
(C) potato and cheese
(D) chicken and cheese

21. Who did NOT like the movie?

(A) the boy
(B) the boy's brother
(C) the boy's mother
(D) the boy's father

[22-23]

22. How long did it take for Chaser to learn over 1,000 words?

(A) 1,728 days
(B) 1,022 days
(C) 3 months
(D) 3 years

23. What kind of animal is Puck?

(A) a dolphin
(B) a bird
(C) an elephant
(D) a dog

[24-25]

24. What did John do at the talent show?

(A) sing
(B) dance
(C) play the cello
(D) play the violin

25. Who played music together?

(A) the boy and John
(B) the boy and Kate
(C) Kate and Susan
(D) John and Susan

PART D Listen and Speak

Directions: You will hear conversations in English. They will be spoken TWICE. After you listen to the conversations, read each question and choose the best response to what the last speaker says.

지시사항 26번부터 30번까지는 대화를 영어로 **두 번** 듣고, 대화의 마지막 질문이나 마지막 말 뒤에 이어질 가장 알맞은 응답을 주어진 질문에 맞게 고르는 문제입니다. D

26. What's next?

(A) But I don't like apples.

(B) But you can't cook.

(C) That's very funny.

(D) That's too spicy.

27. What's next?

(A) Okay, I will.

(B) I caught a cold.

(C) Yes, you're clean.

(D) I'll call the doctor.

28. What's next?

(A) That's good to know.

(B) Great idea!

(C) No problem.

(D) Sure, why not?

29. What's next?

(A) I was tired.

(B) I was late.

(C) I was loud.

(D) I was ready.

30. What's next?

(A) It's at 4:00.

(B) It's far from here.

(C) It's ballet.

(D) It's very fun.

Section II

Reading and Writing

Part **A** ***Sentence Completion***
5 Questions

Part **B** ***Situational Writing***
5 Questions

Part **C** ***Practical Reading and Retelling***
15 Questions

Part **D** ***General Reading and Retelling***
5 Questions

PART A Sentence Completion

Directions: You will see conversations with blanks. Read carefully and choose the one which best completes the blanks.

지시사항 1번에서 5번까지는 빈칸을 알맞게 채워 대화를 완성하는 문제입니다. 가장 알맞은 답을 고르세요.

1. A: Which kite in the sky is yours?

B: ________ red one is mine.

(A) There
(B) That
(C) These
(D) Those

2. A: What did your father say?

B: He ________ me to study harder.

(A) asked
(B) ask
(C) asking
(D) to ask

3. A: Is Jeff still ________?

B: Yes, let's go wake him up.

(A) sleep
(B) sleeping
(C) will sleep
(D) to sleeping

4. A: ________ did you buy that ring?

B: Two days ago.

(A) Why
(B) How
(C) When
(D) What

5. A: We don't have ________ time.

B: Let's hurry.

(A) few
(B) many
(C) much
(D) little

PART B Situational Writing

Directions: You will see pictures and incomplete sentences. Choose the one which best completes the sentences.

지시사항 6번부터 10번까지는 그림을 보고 문장을 완성하는 문제입니다. 가장 알맞은 답을 고르세요.

6.

Her pockets are ____________________.

(A) on the knees of her pants

(B) on the back of her pants

(C) on the sides of her jacket

(D) on the front of her skirt

7.

The man is ____________________.

(A) swimming in the water

(B) jumping over the waves

(C) running out of the ocean

(D) sitting on the beach

8.

The woman is ________________.

(A) crying into a tissue

(B) reading a book

(C) setting the table

(D) blowing her nose

9.

The mother feels __________.

(A) angry

(B) happy

(C) sleepy

(D) worried

10.

The firefighter is saving the cat ________.

(A) from the top of the tree

(B) from under the tree

(C) from beneath the tree

(D) from out of the tree

PART C Practical Reading and Retelling

Directions: You will see practical reading materials. Each reading material is followed by questions about it. Choose the best answer to each question.

지시사항 11번부터 20번까지는 실용적 읽기자료에 관련된 문제입니다. 각 읽기자료 다음에는 질문이 제시됩니다. 각 질문에 해당하는 가장 알맞은 답을 고르세요.

For questions 11 – 12, refer to the following information.

Valentine's Day Party Sign Up

Which food item will you bring to the party?
Write your name next to the food item.

Food Item	Name
Vegetable Plate	Maya, Jason
Pizza	Peter, Tom
Chicken Wings	Brenda, David
Cookies	Loretta, Bobby
Juice and Cups	Doug, James
Plates, Forks, and Spoons	Susan

11. Who will bring chicken wings?

(A) Loretta and Bobby

(B) Maya and Jason

(C) Brenda and David

(D) Peter and Tom

12. Which things will only one person be bringing?

(A) forks and spoons

(B) cups and plates

(C) vegetables and cookies

(D) pizza and chicken

For questions 13 – 14, refer to the following information.

13. How long will the walk day last?

(A) two hours

(B) six and a half hours

(C) twelve hours

(D) twenty-four hours

14. Who will get a prize?

(A) the fastest walkers

(B) the farthest walkers

(C) the healthiest walkers

(D) the earliest walkers

For questions 15 – 16, refer to the following information.

Cost of Hair Styling

	Haircut	Shampoo	Blow-dry
Men	$15.00	$5.00	$3.00
Women	$20.00	$5.00	$5.00
Children	$10.00	$3.00	$3.00

15. How much is it for a children's haircut?

(A) $10.00

(B) $13.00

(C) $15.00

(D) $16.00

16. What can a woman get for thirty dollars?

(A) only a haircut

(B) only a shampoo

(C) only a haircut and blow-dry

(D) a haircut, shampoo, and blow-dry

For question 17 – 18, refer to the following information.

Men's Figure Skating Competition Scores

Place	Name	Country	Points
1st	Patrick Chan	Canada	239.52
2nd	Nobunari Oda	Japan	236.52
3rd	Adam Rippon	United States	233.04
4th	Kevin Reynolds	Canada	218.65

17. How many points did the American get?

(A) 239.52

(B) 236.52

(C) 233.04

(D) 218.65

18. Who came in second place?

(A) Kevin Reynolds

(B) Nobunari Oda

(C) Patrick Chan

(D) Adam Rippon

For question 19 - 20, refer to the following information.

How to Make Eggshell Chalk

This chalk is for sidewalk drawing. Do not use it for chalkboards.

You will need:
* the shells of 6 eggs
* 1 spoon of hot water
* 1 spoon of flour
* food coloring

Break the eggshells to make a powder.
Put 1 spoon of powder in a cup.
Add the flour and hot water. Then, add food coloring.
Shape it into a stick. Let it dry for 3 days.

19. What is this chalk for?

(A) drawing on windows

(B) drawing on chalkboards

(C) drawing on streets

(D) drawing on paper

20. What do you add last to the eggshell powder?

(A) water

(B) flour

(C) eggs

(D) food coloring

PART D General Reading and Retelling

Directions: You will see various reading materials. Each reading material is followed by questions about it. Choose the best answer to each question.

지시사항 21번부터 30번까지는 다양한 읽기 자료에 관련된 문제입니다. 각 읽기 자료 다음에는 질문이 제시됩니다. 각 질문에 해당하는 가장 알맞은 답을 고르세요.

For questions 21 – 22, refer to the following passage.

Burj Khalifa is the world's tallest building. It was built in Dubai, United Arab Emirates. It took 5 years and 6 months to build it. The tower opened on January 4th, 2010. The tower is 828 meters tall. It has 163 floors. It takes about one minute to reach the top riding the elevator.

21. How tall is Burj Khalifa?

(A) 101 meters

(B) 163 meters

(C) 509 meters

(D) 828 meters

22. When did work start to build Burj Khalifa?

(A) in 2004

(B) in 2006

(C) in 2008

(D) in 2010

For questions 23 – 24, refer to the following passage.

The Sun is a middle-aged star. It is the closest star to the Earth. It is 150 million kilometers from the Earth. Alpha Centauri is the next closest star. Sunlight takes just over eight minutes to reach us, but light from Alpha Centauri takes about four years to reach us.

23. How long does it take for light to reach Earth from Alpha Centauri?

(A) about 4 minutes

(B) about 8 minutes

(C) about 4 years

(D) about 8 years

24. What is Alpha Centauri?

(A) the Sun

(B) a moon

(C) a planet

(D) a star

For questions 25 – 26, refer to the following passage.

Sophie Tucker is a gray and black dog. One day Sophie fell off her family's boat. There were many sharks in the ocean, but Sophie was okay. She swam ten kilometers to a small island. She lived there for four months. Finally, someone saw her and helped her. Sophie is now back with her family.

25. Where did Sophie Tucker live for 4 months?

(A) at her family's home

(B) on an island

(C) on a boat

(D) in the ocean

26. How did Sophie Tucker get back home?

(A) She swam home.

(B) She walked home.

(C) Someone helped her.

(D) Her family found her.

For questions 27 – 28, refer to the following passage.

There are five things I really don't like. Number one: I don't like dropping my ice cream cone. Number two: I don't like visiting the dentist. Number three: I don't like getting a haircut. Number four: I don't like missing the school bus. Number five: I hate smelling my brother's stinky socks.

27. What is something the writer really doesn't like?

(A) missing the subway

(B) cooking meals

(C) visiting the dentist

(D) doing the laundry

28. What is the third thing the writer hates?

(A) getting a haircut

(B) dropping ice cream

(C) smelling stinky socks

(D) missing the school bus

For questions 29 – 30, refer to the following passage.

Cooks in the Middle Ages had rules about food. They thought people should eat light foods before heavy foods. So, people ate melons or grapes before meat. Then the stomach was ready to eat heavy foods. Cheese was the heaviest food, so people ate it at the end of meals.

29. Which of the following is the "heaviest" food?

(A) watermelon

(B) meat

(C) grapes

(D) cheese

30. Which are NOT light foods?

(A) melons

(B) meats

(C) oranges

(D) grapes

Appendix

A

across	prep. 건너서, 가로질러
act	v. 연기하다
actually	ad. 실제로
address	n. 주소
afraid	adj. ~을 두려워하는
afterwards	ad. 나중에, 그 뒤에
all the way to	~ 오는 길 내내
alone	ad. 홀로
aloud	ad. 큰 소리로
always	ad. 항상
amusement park	n. 놀이공원
Arctic Ocean	n. 북극해
attic	n. 다락방
average	adj. 평균의
awake	adj. 깨어 있는

B

bamboo	n. 대나무
basement	n. 지하
bat	n. 박쥐
bark	n. 나무 껍질
bath tub	n. 목욕통
be used to	~에 익숙하다
beach	n. 바닷가, 해변
beauty	n. 아름다움
begin	v. 시작하다
beside	prep. 옆에
begin	v. 시작하다
bike	n. 자전거
bison	n. 들소
bite	v. 물다
blond	adj. 금발의
blonde	n. 금발
blow	v. (입으로) 불다
borrow	v. 빌리다
bowl	v. 볼링을 치다
brush	n. 붓
bubble	n. 거품
build	v. (건물을) 짓다
busy	adj. 바쁜
button	n. 단추
buzzing	adj. 윙윙거리는

C

cafeteria	n. 구내식당
cage	n. 새장
camel	n. 낙타
cancel	v. 취소하다
cartoon	n. 만화

castle	n. 성
catcher	n. (야구) 포수
cat nap	n. 토막잠
celebrate	v. 축하하다, 기념하다
chalk	n. 분필
cheap	adj. 싼
cheek	n. 볼, 뺨
chess	n. 체스, 장기
chin	n. 턱
Chinese	n. 중국어
clear off	치우다
climb	v. 오르다, 올라가다
closet	n. 옷장
collect	v. 수집하다
competition	n. 경쟁, 대회
cost	v. 비용이 들다
count	v. 세다
cry into	~에 얼굴을 묻고 울다
cupboard	n. 찬장

D

dangerous	adj. 위험한
decide	v. 결심하다
delicious	adj. 맛있는
dentist	n. 치과 의사
dining	n. 식사
dirty	adj. 더러운
dolphin	n. 돌고래
downtown	n. 시내
draw	v. (그림을) 그리다
drug store	n. 약국
dry off	v. 말리다

E

each other	pron. 서로
early	adj. 이른
eggshell	n. 계란껍질
elbow	n. 팔꿈치
end	v. 끝나다
eyebrow	n. 눈썹

F

fair	n. 축제
famous	adj. 유명한
fan	n. 선풍기
fastest	adj. 가장 빠른
favorite	adj. 가장 좋아하는
fee	n. 요금
feed	v. 먹이를 주다
fell	v. 떨어졌다, 감소했다
field	n. 들판, 운동장

fill	v. 채우다
film-making	n. 영상 제작
find	v. 찾다, 발견하다
fine	adj. 좋은
finish	v. 끝내다
flour	n. 밀가루
fluffy	adj. 솜털로 뒤덮인
food coloring	식용 색소
forget	v. 잊다
freeze	v. 얼다, 얼리다
fresh	adj. 신선한
fridge	n. 냉장고
front	n. 앞면

G

garbage	n. 쓰레기
garden	n. 정원
gate	n. 문
giant panda	n. 대왕판다
gift	n. 선물
glass	n. 유리잔
glove	n. 장갑
glue	n. 접착제
go through	v. 관통하다
goldfish	n. 금붕어
grab	v. 붙잡다, 움켜잡다
grade	n. 성적
grass	n. 풀
Greenland	n. 그린란드
Greenlander	n. 그린란드 사람
grocery store	n. 식품점, 슈퍼마켓
guest	n. 손님, 하객
gym	n. 체육관

H

hall	n. 복도
harder	ad. 더 열심히
headache	n. 두통
healthy	adj. 건강한
heart	n. 심장
heavy	adj. 무거운
height	n. 키
help yourself	마음껏 먹어
hide	v. 숨다
hill	n. 언덕
history	n. 역사
hitter	n. (야구) 타자
hole	n. 구멍
homemade	adj. 집에서 만든, 손으로 만든

hometown	n. 고향
how often	얼마나 자주
hurt	v. 아프게 하다, 아프다

I

ill	adj. 병든, 아픈
information	n. 정보
in-home	집에서 하는
insect	n. 곤충
inside	prep. 안에
instead	ad. 대신에
instrument	n. 악기
interesting	adj. 흥미로운, 재미있는
invite	v. 초대하다

J

join	v. 함께 하다

K

kite	n. 연
koala	n. 코알라

L

ladder	n. 사다리
language	n. 언어
laundry	n. 세탁물
laugh	v. 웃다
learn	v. 배우다
leave	v. 떠나다
lick	v. 핥다
lie	v. 눕다
light	adj. 가벼운
loud	adj. (소리가) 큰, 시끄러운
lots of	많은

M

machine	n. 기계
mainly	ad. 주로
make a speech	연설하다
manner	n. 예의, 예절
math	n.수학
meal	n. 식사
meat	n. 고기
medicine	n. 약, 의학
medium	adj. 중간의
middle	n. 중앙, 한가운데
million	n. 백만
mind	v. 언짢아하다
miss	v. 놓치다
money	n. 돈
month	n. 월, 달
moose	n. 무스
mosquito	n. 모기

mostly	ad. 주로, 대체로

N

neighbor	n. 이웃
nest	n. 둥지
next	adj. 옆의
nickname	n. 별명
noise	n. 시끄러운 소리
no problem	(부탁에 대해) 그럼요

O

ocean	n. 바다
offer	v. 제공하다
often	ad. 종종, 자주
only	ad. 오로지, 단지
order	v. 주문하다
ostrich	n. 타조
owl	n. 올빼미, 부엉이

P

Pacific Ocean	n. 태평양
paint	v. (그림물감으로)그리다, 페인트칠을 하다
paper doll	n. 종이 인형
parade	n. 행진
pass	v. 건네주다, 지나가다
pay	v. 지불하다
peach	n. 복숭아
peanut	n. 땅콩
pen pal	n. 펜팔 친구
people	n. 사람들
percentage	n. 백분율, 비율, 퍼센트
perfect	adj. 완벽한
performer	n. 공연하는 사람
pilot	n. 비행기 조종사
plane	n. 비행기
planet	n. 행성
plate	n. 접시
play	n. 연극
playground	n. 놀이터
point	v. ~를 가르키다
pond	n. 연못
popular	adj. 인기있는
position	n. 위치
pot	n. 냄비
practice	v. 연습하다
prefer	v. 선호하다
prepare	v. 준비하다
present	n. 선물
press	v. 누르다
prize	n. 상

R

race	n. 경주
rarely	ad. 드물게, 거의 ~ 않다
rate	n. 요금
reach one's goal	목표를 이루다
recipe	n. 요리법
record	n. 기록
red panda	n. 너구리 판다
rest	v. 쉬다
restroom	n. 화장실
restaurant	n. 식당
return	v. 돌려주다
rhino	n. 코뿔소
ring	v. 울리다
roof	n. 지붕
rubber	n. 고무
run out of	~로부터 달아나다

S

sand	n. 모래
scared	adj. 무서워하는, 겁먹은
schedule	n. 시간표, 일정표
science	n. 과학
score	n. 점수
seed	n. 씨앗
set up	v. 조율하다, 예약하다
sewing shop	n. 바느질 가게
share	v. 나누다
shark	n. 상어
sharp	adj. 날카로운
shout	v. 소리지르다
sidewalk	n. 보도, 인도
single	adj. 하나의
sink	n. 세면대, 싱크대
slide	n. 미끄럼틀
smart	adj. 똑똑한
smoothly	ad. 순조롭게
snack	n. 간식
snake	n. 뱀
snowball fight	n. 눈싸움
soap	n. 비누
soft	adj. 부드러운
space	n. 우주
special	adj. 특별한
spell	v. (어떤 단어의) 철자를 말하다[쓰다]
spend	v. 보내다, (돈을) 쓰다
spicy	adj. 매운
splash	v. 물속에서 첨벙거리다

sports store	n. 운동 용품 가게
spot	n. 얼룩
stamp	n. 우표
stomach	n. (사람의) 배, 위
stomachache	n. 복통
stinky	adj. 냄새 나는
string	n. 끈, 줄
suddenly	ad. 갑자기
sunshine	n. 햇빛
sweater	n. 스웨터
swing	n. 그네

T

talent	n. 재능
talent show	n. 탤런트 쇼
taller	adj. 더 큰
take a break	쉬다
take a rest	휴식을 취하다, 쉬다
take a seat	자리에 앉다
take one's turn	교대하다, 자기 순서를 맞다
than	~보다
thick	adj. 두꺼운
thirsty	adj. 목이 마른
though	ad. 그러나
throw	v. 던지다
tower	n. 탑, 타워
track	n. (사람들이 걸어다녀서 생긴) 길
triangle	n. 삼각형
trip	n. 여행
trunk	n. (코끼리 등의) 코
tub	n. 욕조
turn	v. 나이가 ~가 되다
twin	n. 쌍둥이

V

vegetable	n. 야채

W

wave	n. 파도
weather	n. 날씨, 기상, 일기
web	n. 거미줄
weight	n. 몸무게
what is A like?	A는 어때?
whole	adj. 전체의, 모든

Y

young	adj. (나이가) 어린, 젊은

국제영어능력인증시험 (TOSEL)

* 연습을 위한 OMR 카드 샘플입니다.

BASIC

한글이름		감독확인	

수 험 번 호

(1)				–				–						
(2)	⓪①②③④⑤⑥⑦⑧⑨	⓪①②③④⑤⑥⑦⑧⑨	⓪①②③④⑤⑥⑦⑧⑨	–	⓪①②③④⑤⑥⑦⑧⑨	⓪①②③④⑤⑥⑦⑧⑨	⓪①②③④⑤⑥⑦⑧⑨	–	⓪①②③④⑤⑥⑦⑧⑨	⓪①②③④⑤⑥⑦⑧⑨	⓪①②③④⑤⑥⑦⑧⑨	⓪①②③④⑤⑥⑦⑧⑨	⓪①②③④⑤⑥⑦⑧⑨	⓪①②③④⑤⑥⑦⑧⑨

주의사항

1. 수험번호 및 답안은 검은색 사인펜을 사용해서 <보기>와 같이 표기합니다.
   <보기> 바른표기 : ● 틀린표기 : ✓ ⊗ ⊙ ◑ ◎
2. 수험번호(1)에는 아라비아 숫자로 쓰고, (2)에는 해당란에 ● 표기합니다.
3. 답안 수정은 수정 테이프로 흔적을 깨끗이 지웁니다.
4. 수험번호 및 답안 작성란 이외의 여백에 낙서를 하지 마시기 바랍니다. 이로 인한 불이익은 수험자 본인 책임입니다.
5. 마킹오류로 채점 불가능한 답안은 0점 처리되오니, 이점 유의하시기 바랍니다.

SECTION Ⅰ

문항	A	B	C	D	문항	A	B	C	D
1	Ⓐ	Ⓑ	Ⓒ	Ⓓ	16	Ⓐ	Ⓑ	Ⓒ	Ⓓ
2	Ⓐ	Ⓑ	Ⓒ	Ⓓ	17	Ⓐ	Ⓑ	Ⓒ	Ⓓ
3	Ⓐ	Ⓑ	Ⓒ	Ⓓ	18	Ⓐ	Ⓑ	Ⓒ	Ⓓ
4	Ⓐ	Ⓑ	Ⓒ	Ⓓ	19	Ⓐ	Ⓑ	Ⓒ	Ⓓ
5	Ⓐ	Ⓑ	Ⓒ	Ⓓ	20	Ⓐ	Ⓑ	Ⓒ	Ⓓ
6	Ⓐ	Ⓑ	Ⓒ	Ⓓ	21	Ⓐ	Ⓑ	Ⓒ	Ⓓ
7	Ⓐ	Ⓑ	Ⓒ	Ⓓ	22	Ⓐ	Ⓑ	Ⓒ	Ⓓ
8	Ⓐ	Ⓑ	Ⓒ	Ⓓ	23	Ⓐ	Ⓑ	Ⓒ	Ⓓ
9	Ⓐ	Ⓑ	Ⓒ	Ⓓ	24	Ⓐ	Ⓑ	Ⓒ	Ⓓ
10	Ⓐ	Ⓑ	Ⓒ	Ⓓ	25	Ⓐ	Ⓑ	Ⓒ	Ⓓ
11	Ⓐ	Ⓑ	Ⓒ	Ⓓ	26	Ⓐ	Ⓑ	Ⓒ	Ⓓ
12	Ⓐ	Ⓑ	Ⓒ	Ⓓ	27	Ⓐ	Ⓑ	Ⓒ	Ⓓ
13	Ⓐ	Ⓑ	Ⓒ	Ⓓ	28	Ⓐ	Ⓑ	Ⓒ	Ⓓ
14	Ⓐ	Ⓑ	Ⓒ	Ⓓ	29	Ⓐ	Ⓑ	Ⓒ	Ⓓ
15	Ⓐ	Ⓑ	Ⓒ	Ⓓ	30	Ⓐ	Ⓑ	Ⓒ	Ⓓ

SECTION Ⅱ

문항	A	B	C	D	문항	A	B	C	D
1	Ⓐ	Ⓑ	Ⓒ	Ⓓ	16	Ⓐ	Ⓑ	Ⓒ	Ⓓ
2	Ⓐ	Ⓑ	Ⓒ	Ⓓ	17	Ⓐ	Ⓑ	Ⓒ	Ⓓ
3	Ⓐ	Ⓑ	Ⓒ	Ⓓ	18	Ⓐ	Ⓑ	Ⓒ	Ⓓ
4	Ⓐ	Ⓑ	Ⓒ	Ⓓ	19	Ⓐ	Ⓑ	Ⓒ	Ⓓ
5	Ⓐ	Ⓑ	Ⓒ	Ⓓ	20	Ⓐ	Ⓑ	Ⓒ	Ⓓ
6	Ⓐ	Ⓑ	Ⓒ	Ⓓ	21	Ⓐ	Ⓑ	Ⓒ	Ⓓ
7	Ⓐ	Ⓑ	Ⓒ	Ⓓ	22	Ⓐ	Ⓑ	Ⓒ	Ⓓ
8	Ⓐ	Ⓑ	Ⓒ	Ⓓ	23	Ⓐ	Ⓑ	Ⓒ	Ⓓ
9	Ⓐ	Ⓑ	Ⓒ	Ⓓ	24	Ⓐ	Ⓑ	Ⓒ	Ⓓ
10	Ⓐ	Ⓑ	Ⓒ	Ⓓ	25	Ⓐ	Ⓑ	Ⓒ	Ⓓ
11	Ⓐ	Ⓑ	Ⓒ	Ⓓ	26	Ⓐ	Ⓑ	Ⓒ	Ⓓ
12	Ⓐ	Ⓑ	Ⓒ	Ⓓ	27	Ⓐ	Ⓑ	Ⓒ	Ⓓ
13	Ⓐ	Ⓑ	Ⓒ	Ⓓ	28	Ⓐ	Ⓑ	Ⓒ	Ⓓ
14	Ⓐ	Ⓑ	Ⓒ	Ⓓ	29	Ⓐ	Ⓑ	Ⓒ	Ⓓ
15	Ⓐ	Ⓑ	Ⓒ	Ⓓ	30	Ⓐ	Ⓑ	Ⓒ	Ⓓ

* 정기시험 OMR로 사용이 불가합니다.

국제토셀위원회

국제영어능력인증시험 (TOSEL)

* 연습을 위한 OMR 카드 샘플입니다.

BASIC

한글이름		감독확인	

수험번호

(1)				–				–					
(2)	0	0	0		0	0	0		0	0	0	0	0
	1	1	1		1	1	1		1	1	1	1	1
	2	2	2		2	2	2		2	2	2	2	2
	3	3	3		3	3	3		3	3	3	3	3
	4	4	4		4	4	4		4	4	4	4	4
	5	5	5	–	5	5	5	–	5	5	5	5	5
	6	6	6		6	6	6		6	6	6	6	6
	7	7	7		7	7	7		7	7	7	7	7
	8	8	8		8	8	8		8	8	8	8	8
	9	9	9		9	9	9		9	9	9	9	9

주의사항

1. 수험번호 및 답안은 검은색 사인펜을 사용해서 <보기>와 같이 표기합니다.
   <보기> 바른표기 : ● 틀린표기 : ✓ ⊗ ⊙ ◐ ◉
2. 수험번호(1)에는 아라비아 숫자로 쓰고, (2)에는 해당란에 ● 표기합니다.
3. 답안 수정은 수정 테이프로 흔적을 깨끗이 지웁니다.
4. 수험번호 및 답안 작성란 이외의 여백에 낙서를 하지 마시기 바랍니다. 이로 인한 불이익은 수험자 본인 책임입니다.
5. 마킹오류로 채점 불가능한 답안은 0점 처리되오니, 이점 유의하시기 바랍니다.

* 정기시험 OMR로 사용이 불가합니다.

SECTION Ⅰ

문항	A	B	C	D	문항	A	B	C	D
1	A	B	C	D	16	A	B	C	D
2	A	B	C	D	17	A	B	C	D
3	A	B	C	D	18	A	B	C	D
4	A	B	C	D	19	A	B	C	D
5	A	B	C	D	20	A	B	C	D
6	A	B	C	D	21	A	B	C	D
7	A	B	C	D	22	A	B	C	D
8	A	B	C	D	23	A	B	C	D
9	A	B	C	D	24	A	B	C	D
10	A	B	C	D	25	A	B	C	D
11	A	B	C	D	26	A	B	C	D
12	A	B	C	D	27	A	B	C	D
13	A	B	C	D	28	A	B	C	D
14	A	B	C	D	29	A	B	C	D
15	A	B	C	D	30	A	B	C	D

SECTION Ⅱ

문항	A	B	C	D	문항	A	B	C	D
1	A	B	C	D	16	A	B	C	D
2	A	B	C	D	17	A	B	C	D
3	A	B	C	D	18	A	B	C	D
4	A	B	C	D	19	A	B	C	D
5	A	B	C	D	20	A	B	C	D
6	A	B	C	D	21	A	B	C	D
7	A	B	C	D	22	A	B	C	D
8	A	B	C	D	23	A	B	C	D
9	A	B	C	D	24	A	B	C	D
10	A	B	C	D	25	A	B	C	D
11	A	B	C	D	26	A	B	C	D
12	A	B	C	D	27	A	B	C	D
13	A	B	C	D	28	A	B	C	D
14	A	B	C	D	29	A	B	C	D
15	A	B	C	D	30	A	B	C	D

국제토셀위원회

국제영어능력인증시험 (TOSEL)

* 연습을 위한 OMR 카드 샘플입니다.

BASIC

한글이름		감독확인	

수 험 번 호

(1)				–				–						
(2)	0	0	0	–	0	0	0	–	0	0	0	0	0	0
	1	1	1		1	1	1		1	1	1	1	1	1
	2	2	2		2	2	2		2	2	2	2	2	2
	3	3	3		3	3	3		3	3	3	3	3	3
	4	4	4		4	4	4		4	4	4	4	4	4
	5	5	5		5	5	5		5	5	5	5	5	5
	6	6	6		6	6	6		6	6	6	6	6	6
	7	7	7		7	7	7		7	7	7	7	7	7
	8	8	8		8	8	8		8	8	8	8	8	8
	9	9	9		9	9	9		9	9	9	9	9	9

주의사항

1. 수험번호 및 답안은 검은색 사인펜을 사용해서 <보기>와 같이 표기합니다.
   <보기> 바른표기 : ● 틀린표기 : ✓ ⊗ ⊙ ◑ ◉
2. 수험번호(1)에는 아라비아 숫자로 쓰고, (2)에는 해당란에 ● 표기합니다.
3. 답안 수정은 수정 테이프로 흔적을 깨끗이 지웁니다.
4. 수험번호 및 답안 작성란 이외의 여백에 낙서를 하지 마시기 바랍니다. 이로 인한 불이익은 수험자 본인 책임입니다.
5. 마킹오류로 채점 불가능한 답안은 0점 처리되오니, 이점 유의하시기 바랍니다.

SECTION Ⅰ

문항	A	B	C	D	문항	A	B	C	D
1	A	B	C	D	16	A	B	C	D
2	A	B	C	D	17	A	B	C	D
3	A	B	C	D	18	A	B	C	D
4	A	B	C	D	19	A	B	C	D
5	A	B	C	D	20	A	B	C	D
6	A	B	C	D	21	A	B	C	D
7	A	B	C	D	22	A	B	C	D
8	A	B	C	D	23	A	B	C	D
9	A	B	C	D	24	A	B	C	D
10	A	B	C	D	25	A	B	C	D
11	A	B	C	D	26	A	B	C	D
12	A	B	C	D	27	A	B	C	D
13	A	B	C	D	28	A	B	C	D
14	A	B	C	D	29	A	B	C	D
15	A	B	C	D	30	A	B	C	D

SECTION Ⅱ

문항	A	B	C	D	문항	A	B	C	D
1	A	B	C	D	16	A	B	C	D
2	A	B	C	D	17	A	B	C	D
3	A	B	C	D	18	A	B	C	D
4	A	B	C	D	19	A	B	C	D
5	A	B	C	D	20	A	B	C	D
6	A	B	C	D	21	A	B	C	D
7	A	B	C	D	22	A	B	C	D
8	A	B	C	D	23	A	B	C	D
9	A	B	C	D	24	A	B	C	D
10	A	B	C	D	25	A	B	C	D
11	A	B	C	D	26	A	B	C	D
12	A	B	C	D	27	A	B	C	D
13	A	B	C	D	28	A	B	C	D
14	A	B	C	D	29	A	B	C	D
15	A	B	C	D	30	A	B	C	D

* 정기시험 OMR로 사용이 불가합니다.

국제토셀위원회

국제영어능력인증시험 (TOSEL)

* 연습을 위한 OMR 카드 샘플입니다.

BASIC

한글이름		감독확인	

수 험 번 호

(1)				–				–						
(2)	0	0	0	–	0	0	0	–	0	0	0	0	0	0
	1	1	1		1	1	1		1	1	1	1	1	1
	2	2	2		2	2	2		2	2	2	2	2	2
	3	3	3		3	3	3		3	3	3	3	3	3
	4	4	4		4	4	4		4	4	4	4	4	4
	5	5	5		5	5	5		5	5	5	5	5	5
	6	6	6		6	6	6		6	6	6	6	6	6
	7	7	7		7	7	7		7	7	7	7	7	7
	8	8	8		8	8	8		8	8	8	8	8	8
	9	9	9		9	9	9		9	9	9	9	9	9

주의사항

1. 수험번호 및 답안은 검은색 사인펜을 사용해서 <보기>와 같이 표기합니다.
   <보기> 바른표기 : ● 틀린표기 : ✓ ⊗ ⊙ ◑ ◉
2. 수험번호(1)에는 아라비아 숫자로 쓰고, (2)에는 해당란에 ● 표기합니다.
3. 답안 수정은 수정 테이프로 흔적을 깨끗이 지웁니다.
4. 수험번호 및 답안 작성란 이외의 여백에 낙서를 하지 마시기 바랍니다. 이로 인한 불이익은 수험자 본인 책임입니다.
5. 마킹오류로 채점 불가능한 답안은 0점 처리되오니, 이점 유의하시기 바랍니다.

* 정기시험 OMR로 사용이 불가합니다.

SECTION Ⅰ

문항	A	B	C	D	문항	A	B	C	D
1	A	B	C	D	16	A	B	C	D
2	A	B	C	D	17	A	B	C	D
3	A	B	C	D	18	A	B	C	D
4	A	B	C	D	19	A	B	C	D
5	A	B	C	D	20	A	B	C	D
6	A	B	C	D	21	A	B	C	D
7	A	B	C	D	22	A	B	C	D
8	A	B	C	D	23	A	B	C	D
9	A	B	C	D	24	A	B	C	D
10	A	B	C	D	25	A	B	C	D
11	A	B	C	D	26	A	B	C	D
12	A	B	C	D	27	A	B	C	D
13	A	B	C	D	28	A	B	C	D
14	A	B	C	D	29	A	B	C	D
15	A	B	C	D	30	A	B	C	D

SECTION Ⅱ

문항	A	B	C	D	문항	A	B	C	D
1	A	B	C	D	16	A	B	C	D
2	A	B	C	D	17	A	B	C	D
3	A	B	C	D	18	A	B	C	D
4	A	B	C	D	19	A	B	C	D
5	A	B	C	D	20	A	B	C	D
6	A	B	C	D	21	A	B	C	D
7	A	B	C	D	22	A	B	C	D
8	A	B	C	D	23	A	B	C	D
9	A	B	C	D	24	A	B	C	D
10	A	B	C	D	25	A	B	C	D
11	A	B	C	D	26	A	B	C	D
12	A	B	C	D	27	A	B	C	D
13	A	B	C	D	28	A	B	C	D
14	A	B	C	D	29	A	B	C	D
15	A	B	C	D	30	A	B	C	D

국제토셀위원회

국제영어능력인증시험 (TOSEL)

* 연습을 위한 OMR 카드 샘플입니다.

BASIC

한글이름		감독확인	

수 험 번 호

(1)				–				–						
(2)	0	0	0		0	0	0		0	0	0	0	0	0
	1	1	1		1	1	1		1	1	1	1	1	1
	2	2	2		2	2	2		2	2	2	2	2	2
	3	3	3		3	3	3		3	3	3	3	3	3
	4	4	4		4	4	4		4	4	4	4	4	4
	5	5	5	–	5	5	5	–	5	5	5	5	5	5
	6	6	6		6	6	6		6	6	6	6	6	6
	7	7	7		7	7	7		7	7	7	7	7	7
	8	8	8		8	8	8		8	8	8	8	8	8
	9	9	9		9	9	9		9	9	9	9	9	9

주의사항

1. 수험번호 및 답안은 검은색 사인펜을 사용해서 <보기>와 같이 표기합니다.
   <보기> 바른표기 : ● 틀린표기 : ✓ ⊗ ⊙ ◑ ◉
2. 수험번호(1)에는 아라비아 숫자로 쓰고, (2)에는 해당란에 ● 표기합니다.
3. 답안 수정은 수정 테이프로 흔적을 깨끗이 지웁니다.
4. 수험번호 및 답안 작성란 이외의 여백에 낙서를 하지 마시기 바랍니다. 이로 인한 불이익은 수험자 본인 책임입니다.
5. 마킹오류로 채점 불가능한 답안은 0점 처리되오니, 이점 유의하시기 바랍니다.

* 정기시험 OMR로 사용이 불가합니다.

SECTION Ⅰ

문항	A	B	C	D	문항	A	B	C	D
1	A	B	C	D	16	A	B	C	D
2	A	B	C	D	17	A	B	C	D
3	A	B	C	D	18	A	B	C	D
4	A	B	C	D	19	A	B	C	D
5	A	B	C	D	20	A	B	C	D
6	A	B	C	D	21	A	B	C	D
7	A	B	C	D	22	A	B	C	D
8	A	B	C	D	23	A	B	C	D
9	A	B	C	D	24	A	B	C	D
10	A	B	C	D	25	A	B	C	D
11	A	B	C	D	26	A	B	C	D
12	A	B	C	D	27	A	B	C	D
13	A	B	C	D	28	A	B	C	D
14	A	B	C	D	29	A	B	C	D
15	A	B	C	D	30	A	B	C	D

SECTION Ⅱ

문항	A	B	C	D	문항	A	B	C	D
1	A	B	C	D	16	A	B	C	D
2	A	B	C	D	17	A	B	C	D
3	A	B	C	D	18	A	B	C	D
4	A	B	C	D	19	A	B	C	D
5	A	B	C	D	20	A	B	C	D
6	A	B	C	D	21	A	B	C	D
7	A	B	C	D	22	A	B	C	D
8	A	B	C	D	23	A	B	C	D
9	A	B	C	D	24	A	B	C	D
10	A	B	C	D	25	A	B	C	D
11	A	B	C	D	26	A	B	C	D
12	A	B	C	D	27	A	B	C	D
13	A	B	C	D	28	A	B	C	D
14	A	B	C	D	29	A	B	C	D
15	A	B	C	D	30	A	B	C	D

국제토셀위원회

Reading Series

내신과 **토셀 고득점**을 한꺼번에

Pre-Starter | Starter | Basic | Junior | High-Junior

- 각 단원 학습 도입부에 주제와 관련된 이미지를 통한 말하기 연습
- 각 Unit 별 4-6개의 목표 단어 제시, 그림 또는 영문으로 단어 뜻을 제공하여 독해 학습 전 단어 숙지
- 독해&실용문 연습을 위한 지문과 Comprehension 문항을 10개씩 수록하여 이해도 확인 및 진단
- 숙지한 독해 지문을 원어민 음성으로 들으며 듣기 학습 , 듣기 전, 듣기 중, 듣기 후 학습 커리큘럼 마련

Listening Series

한국 학생들에게 최적화된 듣기 실력 완성!

Pre-Starter | Starter | Basic | Junior | High-Junior

- 초등 / 중등 교과과정 연계 말하기&듣기 학습과 세분화된 레벨
- TOSEL 기출 문장과 실생활에 자주 활용되는 문장 패턴을 통해 듣기 및 말하기 학습
- 실제 TOSEL 지문의 예문을 활용한 실용적 학습 제공
- 실전 감각 향상과 점검을 위한 기출 문제 수록

Speaking Series

한국 학생들에게 최적화된 말하기 실력 완성!

Pre-Starter | Starter | Basic | Junior | High-Junior

- 단어 → 문법 → 표현 → 대화로 이어지는 단계적인 학습
- 교과과정에 연계한 설계로 내신과 수행평가 완벽 대비
- 최신 수능 출제 문항을 반영한 문장으로 수능 대비까지
- 전국 Speaking 올림피아드 공식 대비 교재

Grammar Series

체계적인 단계별 **문법 지침서**

Pre-Starter | Starter | Basic | Junior | High-Junior

- 초등 / 중등 교과과정 연계 문법 학습과 세분화된 레벨
- TOSEL 기출 문제 연습과 최신 수능 출제 문법을 포함하여 수능 / 내신 대비 가능
- 이해하기 쉬운 그림, 깔끔하게 정리된 표와 설명, 다양한 문제를 통해 문법 학습
- 실전 감각 향상과 점검을 위한 기출 문제 수록

Voca Series

학년별 꼭 알아야하는 **단어 수록!**

Pre-Starter | Starter | Basic | Junior | High-Junior

- 각 단어 학습 도입부에 주제와 관련된 이미지를 통한 말하기 연습
- TOSEL 시험을 기준으로 빈출 지표를 활용한 예문과 문제 구성
- 실제 TOSEL 지문의 예문을 활용한 실용적 학습 제공
- 실전 감각 향상과 점검을 위한 실전 문제 수록

Story Series

읽는 재미에 실력까지 **동시에!**

Pre-Starter | Starter | Basic | Junior

- 초등 / 중등 교과과정 연계 영어 학습과 세분화된 레벨
- 이야기 지문과 단어를 함께 연결지어 학생들의 독해 능력을 평가
- 이해하기 쉬운 그림, 깔끔하게 정리된 표와 설명, 다양한 문제, 재미있는 스토리를 통한 독해 학습
- 다양한 단계의 문항을 풀어보고 학생들의 읽기, 듣기, 쓰기, 말하기 실력을 집중적으로 향상

국제토셀위원회

TOSEL 실전문제집

BASIC

정답 및 해설

국제 토셀 위원회

TOSEL®
실전문제집

BASIC
정답 및 해설

TOSEL BASIC

실전 1회

Section I Listening and Speaking

1 (A)	2 (A)	3 (A)	4 (C)	5 (B)
6 (B)	7 (A)	8 (A)	9 (A)	10 (C)
11 (D)	12 (C)	13 (A)	14 (B)	15 (A)
16 (A)	17 (C)	18 (A)	19 (B)	20 (C)
21 (A)	22 (C)	23 (A)	24 (A)	25 (B)
26 (A)	27 (A)	28 (B)	29 (B)	30 (B)

Section II Reading and Writing

1 (A)	2 (B)	3 (A)	4 (D)	5 (A)
6 (D)	7 (C)	8 (A)	9 (D)	10 (A)
11 (C)	12 (C)	13 (D)	14 (C)	15 (A)
16 (D)	17 (B)	18 (C)	19 (A)	20 (A)
21 (A)	22 (C)	23 (A)	24 (D)	25 (A)
26 (B)	27 (C)	28 (D)	29 (D)	30 (C)

SECTION I LISTENING AND SPEAKING

Part A. Listen and Recognize (p.11)

1. Boy: The girl has brown hair.
   (A)

해석 소년: 소녀는 갈색 머리를 가지고 있다.
풀이 소녀는 갈색 머리를 가지고 있다고 했으므로 답은 (A)이다.

2. Girl: Mr. Brown is a doctor.
   (A)

해석 소녀: Brown씨는 의사이다.
풀이 의사라고 했으므로 답은 (A)이다.

3. Boy: It's a hot sunny day.
   (A)

해석 소년: 뜨겁고 화창한 날이다.
풀이 화창한 날이라고 했으므로 답은 (A)이다.

4. Girl: Charlie is on the bus.
   (C)

해석 소녀: Charlie는 버스에 있다.
풀이 Charlie가 버스에 있다고 했으므로 답은 (C)이다.

5. Girl: Tony and Sally ride bikes in the park.
   (B)

해석 소녀: Tony와 Sally는 공원에서 자전거를 탄다.
풀이 두 명이 자전거를 타고 있는 그림이 적절하므로 답은 (B)이다.

PART B. Listen and Respond (p.13)

6. Boy: Is today Friday?
   Girl: ________________
   (A) Yesterday.
   (B) No, it's Thursday.
   (C) A long week.
   (D) Tomorrow.

해석 소년: 오늘이 금요일이야?
소녀: ________________
(A) 어제.
(B) 아니, 목요일이야.
(C) 긴 주야.
(D) 내일.
풀이 오늘이 금요일인지 묻고 있으므로 아니라고 대답한 후 다른 요일을 제시한 (B)가 답이다.

7. Girl: When is your birthday?
   Boy: ________________
   (A) It's on May 10th.
   (B) I'm ten years old.
   (C) Birthday cake.
   (D) Happy Birthday.

해석 소녀: 생일이 언제야?
소년: ________________
(A) 5월 10일이야.
(B) 난 10살이야.
(C) 생일 케이크.
(D) 생일 축하해.
풀이 생일 날짜를 묻고 있으므로 답은 (A)이다.

8. Boy: Can you help me?
   Girl: ________________
   (A) Yes, I can.
   (B) No, I don't.
   (C) She can't.
   (D) Someone.

해석 소년: 날 도와줄 수 있니?
소녀: ________________
(A) 응, 도와줄 수 있어.
(B) 아니, 나는 안 그래.
(C) 그녀는 할 수 없어.
(D) 누군가.
풀이 소녀의 도움을 요청하고 있으므로 답은 (A)이다.

9. Boy: What's on your desk?
   Girl: ________________
   (A) There's a pencil on my desk.

(B) I have no chair.
(C) My teacher is over there.
(D) It's ready for me.

해석 소녀: 네 책상 위에 무엇이 있니?
소년: ________________
(A) 내 책상 위에는 연필이 있어.
(B) 나는 의자를 갖고 있지 않아.
(C) 내 선생님은 저기에 계셔.
(D) 그것은 날 위해 준비되어 있어.

풀이 책상 위에 무엇이 있는지 물었으므로 답은 (A)이다.

10. Girl: I don't have crayons.
Boy: ________________
(A) It's hot.
(B) I want it.
(C) Have mine.
(D) Thank you.

해석 소녀: 나는 크레파스가 없어.
소년: ________________
(A) 더워.
(B) 난 그것을 원해.
(C) 내 것을 써.
(D) 고마워.

풀이 소녀가 크레파스가 없다고 했으므로 내 것을 쓰라고 한 (C)가 가장 적절하다.

Part C. Listen and Retell (p.14)

11. Boy: Who's on the phone?
Girl: It's my sister Grace.
Question: Who's on the phone?
(D)

해석 소년: 누가 전화했어?
소녀: 내 여동생 Grace야.
질문: 누가 전화를 하고 있습니까?

풀이 여동생 Grace가 전화를 하고 있다고 했으므로 답은 (D)이다.

12. Boy: What color are your flowers?
Girl: They're yellow.
Question: What color are her flowers?
(C)

해석 소년: 네 꽃은 무슨 색이니?
소녀: 노란색이야.
질문: 그녀의 꽃은 무슨 색입니까?

풀이 꽃이 노란색이라고 했으므로 답은 (C)이다.

13. Girl: Where's your pencil?
Boy: It's in my bag.
Question: Where is his pencil?
(A)

해석 소녀: 네 연필 어디있니?
소년: 내 가방 안에 있어.
질문: 그의 연필은 어디 있습니까?

풀이 연필이 가방 안에 있다고 했으므로 답은 (A)이다.

14. Girl: Can they dance?
Boy: No, but they can swim.
Question: What can they do?
(A) ski
(B) swim
(C) sing
(D) dance

해석 소녀: 그들이 춤을 출 수 있니?
소년: 아니, 하지만 수영은 할 수 있어.
질문: 그들은 무엇을 할 수 있습니까?
(A) 스키타다
(B) 수영하다
(C) 노래하다
(D) 춤추다

풀이 그들은 수영을 할 수 있다고 했으므로 답은 (B)이다.

15. Boy: Is it raining?
Girl: No, but it's windy.
Question: What is the weather like?
(A) windy
(B) hot
(C) cold
(D) rainy

해석 소년: 비 와?
소녀: 아니, 하지만 바람이 불어.
질문: 날씨가 어떻습니까?
(A) 바람이 부는
(B) 더운
(C) 추운
(D) 비가 오는

풀이 바람이 분다고 했으므로 답은 (A)이다.

Words and Phrases weather 날씨, 기상, 일기

16. Girl: Do you like pizza?
Boy: Yes, I do. I eat it often.
Question: Does the boy like pizza?
(A) Yes, he does.
(B) Sometimes.
(C) No, he doesn't.
(D) Never.

해석 소녀: 피자를 좋아하니?
소년: 응, 좋아해. 나는 종종 먹어.
질문: 소년은 피자를 좋아합니까?
(A) 네, 그는 좋아합니다.
(B) 가끔.
(C) 아니오, 그는 좋아하지 않습니다.
(D) 절대, 전혀 (~하지 않다).

풀이 그는 피자를 좋아해서 종종 먹는다고 했으므로 답은 (A)이다.

Words and Phrases often 종종, 자주

17. Boy: Do you have English class today?
Girl: No, it's Monday. I have English class tomorrow.
Question: When is her English class?
(A) Friday
(B) Monday
(C) Tuesday
(D) Yesterday

해석 소년: 오늘 영어 수업이 있니?
소녀: 아니, 오늘은 월요일이야. 나는 내일 영어 수업이 있어.
질문: 소녀는 언제 영어 수업이 있습니까?
(A) 금요일
(B) 월요일
(C) 화요일
(D) 어제

풀이 오늘은 월요일이고 내일 영어수업이 있다고 했으므로 답은 (C)이다.

[18–19]
Girl: John's favorite dessert is cake. He really loves his mom's double chocolate fudge cake. On his birthday, his mom always makes two cakes. One for the birthday guests, and one for John to eat all by himself. He always eats the whole thing before he goes to bed.

18. What is John's favorite dessert?
(A) cake
(B) cookies
(C) apples
(D) chicken

19. What kind of cake does his mom make?
(A) vanilla
(B) chocolate
(C) carrot
(D) lemon

해석 소녀: John이 가장 좋아하는 디저트는 케이크다. 그는 그의 엄마의 더블 초콜릿 퍼지 케이크를 정말 좋아한다. 그의 생일날, 그의 엄마는 항상 케이크를 두 개 만든다. 하나는 생일 파티 손님들을 위한 것이고, 다른 하나는 John이 혼자 다 먹기 위한 것이다. 그는 항상 잠자리에 들기 전에 하나를 다 먹는다.

18. John이 가장 좋아하는 디저트는 무엇입니까?
(A) 케이크
(B) 쿠키
(C) 사과
(D) 치킨

19. 그의 엄마는 어떤 종류의 케이크를 만듭니까?
(A) 바닐라
(B) 초콜렛
(C) 당근
(D) 레몬

풀이 John은 케이크를 가장 좋아한다고 했으므로 18번의 답은 (A)이다. 엄마는 항상 초콜릿 퍼지 케이크를 만든다고 했으므로 19번의 답은 (B)이다.

Words and Phrases favorite 마음에 드는, 매우 좋아하는 guest 손님, 하객 whole 전체의, 모든

[20–21]
Boy: Craig has an alarm clock beside his bed. It has big red numbers that he can see even in the dark. When it is time to wake up, the clock makes a loud buzzing noise. Craig always turns his alarm off, so his mother has to come wake him up.

20. How does Craig finally wake up?
(A) His alarm clock rings.
(B) He falls out of the bed.
(C) His mother wakes him up.
(D) He has a bad dream.

21. What color are the numbers?
(A) red
(B) orange
(C) dark
(D) blue

해석 소년: Craig는 침대 옆에 알람 시계가 있다. 그것은 큰 빨간 숫자가 있어서 그가 어둠속에서도 볼 수 있다. 일어날 때가 되면, 시계가 큰 소리를 내며 운다. Craig는 항상 알람을 꺼서, 엄마가 와서 그를 깨워야 한다.

20. Craig는 결국 어떻게 일어납니까?
(A) 그의 알람 시계가 울린다.
(B) 그가 침대 밖으로 떨어진다.
(C) 엄마가 그를 깨운다.
(D) 그는 나쁜 꿈을 꾼다.

21. 숫자는 어떤 색입니까?
(A) 빨간색
(B) 오렌지색
(C) 어두운
(D) 파란색

풀이 마지막에는 엄마가 깨우러 온다고 했으므로 20번의 답은 (C)이다. 숫자는 빨간색이라고 했으므로 21번의 답은 (A)이다.

Words and Phrases beside 옆에 loud (소리가) 큰, 시끄러운

[22–23]
Woman: Tonight, I cooked dinner with my mother, and my sister studied. Mom and I made fried chicken, corn, and potatoes. After we finished eating, my sister washed the dishes, because she didn't cook. I talked with my friends on the phone, and my mom watched TV.

22. What does the speaker do?
(A) watch TV
(B) study
(C) talk on the phone
(D) eat breakfast

23. Who does the dishes?

(A) her sister

(B) her mother

(C) nobody

(D) the speaker

해석 여자: 오늘 밤, 나는 엄마와 저녁을 요리했고 여동생은 공부를 했다. 엄마와 나는 튀긴 치킨, 옥수수, 감자를 만들었다. 다 먹은 이후, 내 여동생은 요리를 하지 않았기 때문에 설거지를 했다. 나는 내 친구와 통화를 했고, 엄마는 TV를 봤다.

22. 화자는 무엇을 합니까?

(A) TV를 본다

(B) 공부한다

(C) 통화한다

(D) 아침을 먹는다

23. 누가 설거지를 합니까?

(A) 그녀의 여동생

(B) 그녀의 어머니

(C) 아무도 안한다

(D) 화자

풀이 화자는 친구와 통화를 했다고 했으므로 22번의 답은 (C)이다. 요리 하지 않은 여동생이 설거지를 했다고 했으므로 23번의 답은 (A)이다.

[24–25]

Girl: Elephants are big animals with long trunks. I like to go to the zoo and look at them with my sister. She is younger than me, so she gets a little scared. She is not used to their large size and loud noises.

24. Where do they see the elephants?

(A) at the zoo

(B) on a safari

(C) in a dream

(D) on the street

25. Who gets scared?

(A) the speaker

(B) the speaker's little sister

(C) the speaker's bigger sister

(D) the speaker's brother

해석 소녀: 코끼리는 긴 코를 가진 큰 동물이다. 나는 동물원에 가서 내 여동생과 함께 그들을 보는 것을 좋아한다. 그녀는 나보다 어려서 조금 겁을 먹는다. 그녀는 그들의 큰 크기와 시끄러운 소리에 익숙하지 않다.

24. 그들은 코끼리를 어디서 봅니까?

(A) 동물원에서

(B) 사파리에서

(C) 꿈에서

(D) 길에서

25. 누가 겁을 먹습니까?

(A) 화자

(B) 화자의 여동생

(C) 화자의 언니

(D) 화자의 남동생

풀이 동물원에서 코끼리를 본다고 했으므로 24번의 답은 (A)이다. 여동생이 겁을 먹는다고 했으므로 25번의 답은 (B)이다.

Words and Phrases trunk (코끼리 등의) 코 be used to ~에 익숙하다
noise 시끄러운 소리 scared 무서워하는, 겁먹은

Part D. Listen and Speak (p.18)

26. Girl: What's this?
Boy: It's a crayon.
Girl: What color is it?
Boy: ____________________

(A) It's red.

(B) It's old.

(C) It's new.

(D) It's broken.

해석 소녀: 이게 뭐야?
소년: 그건 크레파스야.
소녀: 이건 무슨 색이야?
소년: ____________________

(A) 그건 빨간색이야.

(B) 그건 낡았어.

(C) 그건 새 거야.

(D) 그건 망가졌어.

풀이 색깔을 물었으므로 답은 (A)이다.

27. Boy: Where's the tub?
Girl: It's in the bathroom.
Boy: Is there soap in the bathroom?
Girl: ____________________

(A) Yes, it's next to the sink.

(B) No, the bathroom is dirty.

(C) Yes, there's a tower.

(D) No, it's in the bathroom.

해석 소년: 욕조 어디 있어?
소녀: 화장실에 있어.
소년: 화장실에 비누 있어?
소녀: ____________________

(A) 응, 세면대 옆에 있어.

(B) 아니, 화장실은 더러워.

(C) 응, 저기 타워가 있어.

(D) 아니, 화장실에 있어.

풀이 비누가 있는지 물었으므로 답은 (A)이다.

Words and Phrases tub 욕조 tower 탑, 타워 sink 세면대
soap 비누, 비누칠하다

28. Girl: Where do you like to shop?
Boy: I like to shop downtown.
Girl: What's your favorite store?

Boy: ___________________
(A) I don't like to shop.
(B) I like the sports store.
(C) It's a good restaurant.
(D) There are many stores.

해석 소녀: 너는 어디서 쇼핑하는 것을 좋아해?
소년: 나는 시내에서 쇼핑하는 것을 좋아해.
소녀: 네가 가장 좋아하는 가게는 뭐야?
소년: ___________________
(A) 나는 쇼핑하는 것을 안 좋아해.
(B) 나는 운동 용품 가게를 좋아해.
(C) 좋은 레스토랑이야.
(D) 많은 가게들이 있어.

풀이 가장 좋아하는 가게를 물었으므로 가게의 종류로 답한 (B)가 정답이다.

Words and Phrases downtown 시내 sports store 운동 용품 가게

29. Boy: Who is she?
Girl: She's Mrs. Long.
Boy: What does she do?
Girl: ___________________
(A) She's very nice.
(B) She's a doctor.
(C) She's my sister.
(D) She's very old.

해석 소년: 그녀는 누구야?
소녀: 그녀는 Mrs. Long이야.
소년: 그녀의 직업은 무엇이야?
소녀: ___________________
(A) 그녀는 매우 착해.
(B) 그녀는 의사야.
(C) 그녀는 내 여동생이야.
(D) 그녀는 매우 나이가 많아.

풀이 직업을 물었으므로 답은 (B)이다.

30. Boy: I like animals.
Girl: What's your favorite animal?
Boy: I like horses the best.
Girl: ___________________
(A) Yes.
(B) Me, too!
(C) I can't.
(D) It can run.

해석 소년: 나는 동물을 좋아해.
소녀: 가장 좋아하는 동물이 뭐야?
소년: 나는 말을 가장 좋아해.
소녀: ___________________
(A) 응.
(B) 나도!
(C) 나는 할 수 없어.
(D) 그것은 뛸 수 있어.

풀이 가장 좋아하는 동물이 말이라는 소년의 대답에 적절한 반응은 (B)이다.

SECTION II READING AND WRITING

Part A. Sentence Completion (p.21)

1. A: How old are ___________?
B: I am 10 years old.
(A) you
(B) her
(C) she
(D) it

해석 A: **너는** 몇 살이니?
B: 나는 10살이야.
(A) 너
(B) 그녀를, 그녀의
(C) 그녀
(D) 그것

풀이 B가 자신의 나이를 말한 것을 보아 A는 B의 나이를 물었음을 알 수 있다. 따라서 답은 (A)이다.

2. A: Where is the picture?
B: It's ___________ the wall.
(A) in
(B) on
(C) under
(D) with

해석 A: 그림이 어디 있어?
B: 벽 **위에** 있어.
(A) ~안에
(B) ~위에
(C) ~아래
(D) ~와 함께

풀이 보기 중 그림을 벽 위에 걸어놓는 것이 가장 자연스러우므로 답은 (B)이다.

3. A: Do you ___________ lunch?
B: Yes, I'm hungry.
(A) want
(B) wants
(C) wanted
(D) wanting

해석 A: 점심 **먹을래?**
B: 응, 나는 배고파.
(A) 원하다
(B) 원하다(3인칭 단수)
(C) 원했다
(D) 원하는

풀이 'Do'가 주어 앞에 위치한 의문문으로 주어 다음에 동사원형이 나와야 한다. 따라서 답은 (A)이다.

4. A: __________ were you last night?
B: I was with Amy.
(A) Why
(B) Who
(C) When
(D) Where

해석 A: 너 어젯밤 **어디** 있었니?
B: 나 Amy랑 있었어.
(A) 왜
(B) 누구
(C) 언제
(D) 어디

풀이 B의 대답은 장소와 관련 있으므로 '어디'를 물어보는 의문사 where가 적절하다. 따라서 답은 (D)이다.

5. A: Who is coming to the event?
B: Ellen __________ Alex will go there.
(A) or
(B) so
(C) but
(D) because

해석 A: 누가 행사에 올 거니?
B: Ellen **혹은** Alex가 거기 갈 거야.
(A) 혹은
(B) 그래서
(C) 하지만
(D) 왜냐하면

풀이 B는 A의 물음에 두 사람을 언급하고 있으며 문맥 상 Ellen '혹은' Alex가 간다고 말하는 것이 자연스럽다. 따라서 답은 (A)이다.

Part B. Situational Writing (p.22)

6. Her skirt is ________________.
(A) green
(B) red
(C) yellow
(D) blue

해석 그녀의 치마는 **파란색**이다.
(A) 초록색
(B) 빨간색
(C) 노란색
(D) 파란색

풀이 사진의 치마는 파란색이므로 답은 (D)이다.

7. The man is ________________.
(A) cold
(B) young
(C) old
(D) hot

해석 남자는 **나이가 많다**.
(A) 추운
(B) 어린
(C) 나이가 많은
(D) 뜨거운

풀이 그림의 남자는 나이가 많으므로 답은 (C)이다.

8. Her dress is ________________.
(A) too big
(B) too short
(C) too small
(D) green

해석 그녀의 드레스는 **너무 크다**.
(A) 너무 큰
(B) 너무 짧은
(C) 너무 작은
(D) 초록색인

풀이 여자가 너무 큰 드레스를 입고 있으므로 답은 (A)이다.

9. They are ________________.
(A) resting
(B) sleeping
(C) eating
(D) dancing

해석 그들은 **춤추고 있다**.
(A) 쉬다
(B) 자다
(C) 먹다
(D) 춤추다

풀이 사진의 사람들은 춤추고 있으므로 답은 (D)이다.

Words and Phrases rest 쉬다

10. There is a turtle ________________ the pond.
(A) in
(B) behind
(C) above
(D) beside

해석 호수 **안에** 거북이가 있다.
(A) 안에
(B) 뒤에
(C) 위에
(D) 옆에

풀이 호수 안에 거북이가 있으므로 답은 (A)이다.

Words and Phrases pond 연못, 호수

Part C. Practical Reading and Retelling (p.24)

[11–12]

11. Which candy do the children like the most?

(A) hard candy

(B) soft candy

(C) chocolate

(D) gum

12. How many children were asked?

(A) 35

(B) 40

(C) 45

(D) 50

해석 11. 어떤 사탕을 아이들이 가장 좋아합니까?

(A) 딱딱한 사탕

(B) 말랑한 사탕

(C) 초콜릿

(D) 껌

12. 몇 명의 아이들이 질문을 받았습니까?

(A) 35

(B) 40

(C) 45

(D) 50

풀이 초콜릿을 좋아하는 아이가 30명으로 가장 많으므로 11번의 답은 (C)이다. 그래프의 응답한 아이들의 숫자를 다 더하면 45명이므로 12번의 답은 (C)이다.

[13–14]

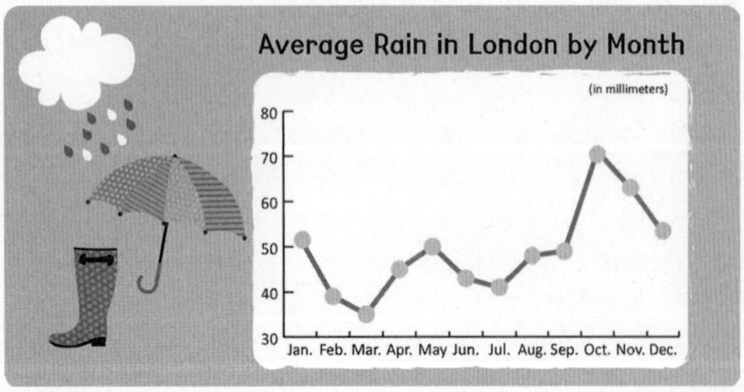

13. In which month does it rain the most?

(A) January

(B) May

(C) July

(D) October

14. Which month has less rain than April?

(A) January

(B) May

(C) July

(D) October

해석 13. 어느 달에 가장 비가 많이 내립니까?

(A) 1월

(B) 5월

(C) 7월

(D) 10월

14. 4월보다 더 적은 비가 내린 달은 언제입니까?

(A) 1월

(B) 5월

(C) 7월

(D) 10월

풀이 그림에서 비가 가장 많이 내린 달을 찾아보면 10월인 것을 알 수 있으므로 답은 (D)이다. 그림에서 4월보다 비가 더 적게 내린 달을 찾아보면 2월, 3월, 6월, 7월이다. 따라서 보기 중 4월보다 비가 적게 내린 달은 7월이므로 답은 (C)이다.

Words and Phrases average 평균의

[15–16]

15. Which of the following animals is the tallest?

(A) ostrich

(B) bear

(C) bison

(D) rhino

16. Which animals are the same size?

(A) elephant and giraffe

(B) buffalo and moose

(C) rhino and horse

(D) bison and bear

해석 15. 다음 중 가장 큰 동물은 무엇입니까?
(A) 타조
(B) 곰
(C) 들소
(D) 코뿔소

16. 크기가 같은 동물은 무엇입니까?
(A) 코끼리와 기린
(B) 버팔로와 무스
(C) 코뿔소와 말
(D) 들소와 곰

풀이 네 보기 중 가장 큰 동물은 타조이므로 15번의 답은 (A)이다.
곰과 들소가 2.1m로 크기가 같으므로 16번의 답은 (D)이다.

Words and Phrases moose 무스 ostrich 타조 camel 낙타 bison 들소 rhino 코뿔소

[17–18]

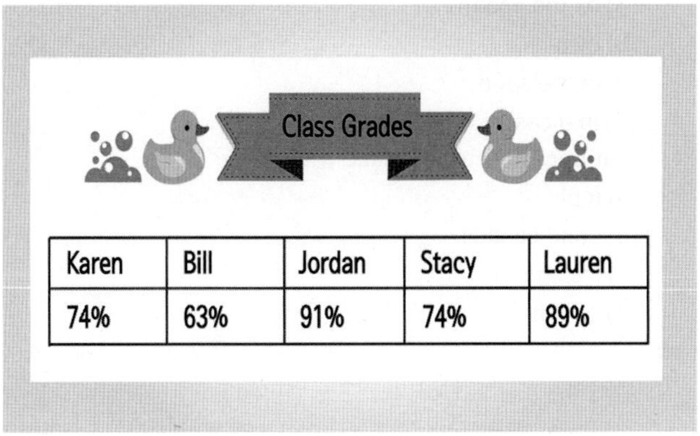

Karen	Bill	Jordan	Stacy	Lauren
74%	63%	91%	74%	89%

17. Who has the worst grades in class?
(A) Karen
(B) Bill
(C) Jordan
(D) Lauren

18. Which two students have the same grades?
(A) Bill and Jordan
(B) Lauren and Jordan
(C) Karen and Stacy
(D) Bill and Lauren

해석 17. 반에서 가장 안 좋은 점수를 받은 사람은 누구입니까?
(A) Karen
(B) Bill
(C) Jordan
(D) Lauren

18. 같은 점수를 받은 두 학생은 누구입니까?
(A) Bill과 Jordan
(B) Lauren과 Jordan
(C) Karen과 Stacy
(D) Bill과 Lauren

풀이 Bill이 63%로 제일 낮으므로 17번의 답은 (B)이다. Karen과 Stacy가 둘 다 74%로 점수가 같으므로 18번의 답은 (C)이다.

[19–20]

Humans	Pigs	Zebra	Deer	Horses	Monkeys	Dogs
5	2	1	2	1	5	4

19. Which animal has the most number of toes on one foot?
(A) monkey
(B) zebra
(C) pig
(D) dog

20. In this list, in what place are humans for most number of toes?
(A) first
(B) second
(C) third
(D) fourth

해석 19. 한 발에 가장 많은 발가락을 가지고 있는 동물은 무엇입니까?
(A) 원숭이
(B) 얼룩말
(C) 돼지
(D) 개

20. 이 표에서, 발가락이 많은 것으로는 인간이 몇 번째입니까?
(A) 첫 번째
(B) 두 번째
(C) 세 번째
(D) 네 번째

풀이 표에서 원숭이와 인간이 5개로 한 발에 가장 많은 발가락을 가지고 있다고 했으므로 19번의 답은 (A)이다. 인간이 원숭이와 함께 한 발에 발가락이 5개로 가장 많으므로 20번의 답은 (A)이다.

Part D. General Reading and Retelling (p.29)

[21–22]
Lions are big animals with sharp teeth. They eat smaller animals for food. They have strong legs and can run very fast. However, they also like to take long cat naps during most of the day. There are no lions in my country, but you can see them at the zoo.

21. What do lions eat?
(A) smaller animals
(B) fruit
(C) vegetables
(D) cake

22. Where can you see lions in the author's country?

(A) on the street

(B) at the supermarket

(C) at the zoo

(D) You cannot see them.

해석 사자는 날카로운 이빨을 가진 큰 동물이다. 그들은 작은 동물들을 먹이로 먹는다. 그들은 튼튼한 다리를 가지고 있고 매우 빠르게 달릴 수 있다. 하지만, 그들은 또한 하루의 대부분을 토막잠을 자는 것을 좋아한다. 우리나라에는 사자가 없지만, 동물원에서 볼 수 있다.

21. 사자는 무엇을 먹습니까?

(A) 작은 동물들

(B) 과일

(C) 야채

(D) 케이크

22. 작가의 나라에서 사자는 어디에서 볼 수 있습니까?

(A) 길거리에서

(B) 슈퍼마켓에서

(C) 동물원에서

(D) 볼 수 없다.

풀이 사자는 작은 동물들을 먹이로 먹는다고 했으므로 21번의 답은 (A)이다. 동물원에서 볼 수 있다고 했으므로 22번의 답은 (C)이다.

Words and Phrases sharp 날카로운 cat nap 토막잠

[23–24]

May is a fun month in Korea. We have a special day just for children. It is called "Children's Day". We gets gifts and candy. We play games and eat our favorite foods. We do not even have to go to school! It is a great day to spend a fun time with our families.

23. Which month is fun in Korea?

(A) May

(B) June

(C) July

(D) August

24. Who is the special day for?

(A) mothers

(B) fathers

(C) teachers

(D) children

해석 5월은 한국에서 즐거운 달이다. 우리는 아이들을 위한 특별한 날이 있다. 그것은 "어린이 날"이라고 불린다. 우리는 선물과 사탕을 받는다. 우리는 게임을 하고 우리가 가장 좋아하는 음식을 먹는다. 우리는 심지어 학교에 가지 않는다! 우리의 가족과 즐거운 시간을 보내기 좋은 날이다.

23. 한국에서 즐거운 달은 언제입니까?

(A) 5월

(B) 6월

(C) 7월

(D) 8월

24. 특별한 날은 누구를 위한 날입니까?

(A) 엄마들

(B) 아빠들

(C) 교사들

(D) 아이들

풀이 5월이 재미있는 달이라고 했으므로 23번의 답은 (A)이다. 어린이를 위한 날이라고 했으므로 24번의 답은 (D)이다.

Words and Phrases spend (시간을) 보내다, (돈을) 쓰다 gift 선물

[25–26]

August is very hot. I live by the ocean, so I love to go swimming. I also like to play in the sand. My sister and I make sand castles. Sometimes, we eat ice cream on the beach. I always get a little sad when summer ends and the weather gets colder.

25. Where does the author live?

(A) by the ocean

(B) by a lake

(C) in the sand

(D) in a castle

26. What does the author make with sister?

(A) tents

(B) sand castles

(C) ice cream

(D) ocean

해석 8월은 매우 뜨겁다. 나는 바다 옆에서 살아서 수영하는 것을 매우 좋아한다. 나는 또한 모래에서 노는 것을 좋아한다. 여동생과 나는 모래 성을 만든다. 가끔, 우리는 해변에서 아이스크림을 먹는다. 나는 여름이 끝나고 날씨가 추워지면 항상 조금 슬퍼진다.

25. 작가는 어디에 삽니까?

(A) 바다 옆에

(B) 호수 옆에

(C) 모래에

(D) 성 안에

26. 작가는 여동생과 무엇을 만듭니까?

(A) 텐트

(B) 모래성

(C) 아이스크림

(D) 바다

풀이 지문에서 바다 옆에 산다고 했으므로 25번의 답은 (A)이다. 여동생과 모래성을 만든다고 했으므로 26번의 답은 (B)이다.

Words and Phrases castle 성

[27–28]

Sam likes his toy robot. It can walk and talk. He takes his robot to school with him. His friends think his robot is very fun. Sam and his friends play with it on the playground. Everyone takes turns sharing the robot, and they all have a fun time.

27. What can Sam's robot do?

(A) sing

(B) write

(C) walk and talk

(D) play and sing

28. Where do Sam and his friends play with his robot?

(A) at the station

(B) at home

(C) in the classroom

(D) on the playground

해석 Sam은 그의 장난감 로봇을 좋아한다. 그것은 걷고 말할 수 있다. 그는 로봇을 학교에 가져간다. 그의 친구들은 로봇이 매우 재미있다고 생각한다. Sam과 그의 친구들은 놀이터에서 그것과 논다. 모두는 돌아가면서 로봇을 나누고, 그들은 모두 즐거운 시간을 보낸다.

27. Sam의 로봇은 무엇을 할 수 있습니까?

(A) 노래하다

(B) 쓰다

(C) 걷고 말하다

(D) 놀고 노래하다

28. Sam과 친구들은 로봇과 어디에서 놉니까?

(A) 역에서

(B) 집에서

(C) 교실에서

(D) 놀이터에서

풀이 로봇은 걷고 말한다고 했으므로 27번의 답은 (C)이다.
아이들은 놀이터에서 논다고 했으므로 28번의 답은 (D)이다.

Words and Phrases playground 놀이터 take turns 교대로 ~을 하다 share 나누다

[29–30]

Judy is making a paper doll. She wants to use glue. Judy looks inside her pencil case. She sees three pencils, two erasers, and a ruler. No glue! Judy looks inside her school bag. She does not see glue, but she finds some tape. She will just use that instead.

29. What is Judy making?

(A) glue

(B) paper

(C) a pencil case

(D) a paper doll

30. Where does Judy find the tape?

(A) on her pencil case

(B) in her pencil case

(C) in her school bag

(D) under her school bag

해석 Judy는 종이 인형을 만들고 있다. 그녀는 풀을 사용하고 싶어한다. Judy는 필통 안을 본다. 그녀는 연필 세 자루, 지우개 두 개, 그리고 자 한 개를 본다. 풀이 없다! 그녀는 책가방 안을 본다. 그녀는 풀을 보지 못하지만 테이프를 찾아낸다. 그녀는 그것을 대신 사용할 것이다.

29. Judy는 무엇을 만들고 있습니까?

(A) 풀

(B) 종이

(C) 필통

(D) 종이 인형

30. Judy는 어디에서 테이프를 찾습니까?

(A) 필통 위에서

(B) 필통 안에서

(C) 책가방 안에서

(D) 책가방 밑에서

풀이 Judy는 종이 인형을 만든다고 했으므로 29번의 답은 (D)이다. 테이프는 책가방 안에서 찾았으므로 30번의 답은 (C)이다.

Words and Phrases paper doll 종이 인형 inside ~안에 instead ~대신

TOSEL BASIC

실전 2회

Section I Listening and Speaking

1 (A)	2 (B)	3 (A)	4 (D)	5 (C)
6 (D)	7 (C)	8 (B)	9 (B)	10 (A)
11 (D)	12 (C)	13 (A)	14 (A)	15 (D)
16 (D)	17 (A)	18 (A)	19 (B)	20 (B)
21 (C)	22 (C)	23 (D)	24 (B)	25 (D)
26 (D)	27 (B)	28 (C)	29 (B)	30 (D)

Section II Reading and Writing

1 (C)	2 (A)	3 (A)	4 (B)	5 (B)
6 (B)	7 (D)	8 (D)	9 (A)	10 (D)
11 (B)	12 (C)	13 (D)	14 (C)	15 (B)
16 (B)	17 (C)	18 (B)	19 (C)	20 (B)
21 (D)	22 (C)	23 (C)	24 (B)	25 (D)
26 (A)	27 (C)	28 (D)	29 (A)	30 (C)

SECTION I LISTENING AND SPEAKING

Part A. Listen and Recognize (p.36)

1. Girl: The elephant has big ears.
(A)
해석 소녀: 코끼리는 큰 귀를 가지고 있다.
풀이 귀가 큰 코끼리 (A)가 답이다.

2. Boy: There are three children sleeping.
(B)
해석 소년: 세 아이가 자고 있다.
풀이 세 아이가 자는 그림 (B)가 답이다.

3. Girl: The boy is next to the tree.
(A)
해석 소녀: 소년이 나무 옆에 있다.
풀이 나무 옆에 서 있는 소년 (A)가 답이다.

4. Boy: The mouse likes cheese.
(D)
해석 소년: 쥐가 치즈를 좋아한다.
풀이 쥐가 치즈를 좋아한다고 했으므로 답은 치즈와 함께 있는 그림 (D)이다.

5. Girl: They go to school on the school bus.
(C)
해석 소녀: 그들은 통학 버스를 타고 학교에 간다.
풀이 통학 버스를 타고 있는 아이들 (C)가 답이다.

PART B. Listen and Respond (p.38)

6. Girl: What are you doing?
Boy: ____________________
(A) I'm sad.
(B) I'm angry.
(C) It's too old.
(D) I'm studying.
해석 소녀: 너 무엇을 하고 있니?
소년: ______________
(A) 나는 슬퍼.
(B) 나는 화가 나.
(C) 그건 너무 낡았어.
(D) 나는 공부하고 있어.
풀이 소년에게 지금 무엇을 하는지 물었으므로 답은 (D)이다.

7. Boy: Where is Mary?
Girl: ____________________
(A) I'm in my room.
(B) We're in the bedroom.
(C) She's in the kitchen.
(D) They're on the moon.
해석 소년: Mary가 어디 있니?
소녀: ______________
(A) 나는 내 방에 있어.
(B) 우리는 침실에 있어.
(C) 그녀는 부엌에 있어.
(D) 그들은 달에 있어.
풀이 Mary의 위치를 물었으므로 답은 (C)이다.

8. Girl: This is my new scarf.
Boy: ____________________
(A) Is it cold?
(B) I think it's pretty.
(C) I need new shoes.
(D) Is there a green brush?
해석 소녀: 이것은 내 새로운 스카프야.
소년: ______________
(A) 추워?
(B) 나는 예쁘다고 생각해.
(C) 나는 새 신발이 필요해.
(D) 초록색 솔이 있니?
풀이 새로운 스카프를 보여주는 소녀의 말에 가장 적절한 대답은 (B)이다.

9. Boy: How often do you clean your room?
Girl: ____________________

(A) For 2 hours.
(B) Once a week.
(C) Nothing.
(D) At home.

해석 소년: 너는 방을 얼마나 자주 치우니?
소녀: ________________
(A) 2시간 동안.
(B) 일주일에 한 번.
(C) 없어.
(D) 집에서.

풀이 소녀에게 얼마나 자주 방을 치우는지 물었으므로 답은 (B)이다.

Words and Phrases how often 얼마나 자주

10. Girl: I think tulips are prettier than roses.
Boy: ________________
(A) I like roses better.
(B) Are you sure?
(C) She likes roses, too.
(D) That's better.

해석 소녀: 나는 튤립이 장미보다 예쁜 것 같아.
소년: ________________
(A) 나는 장미를 더 좋아해.
(B) 확실해?
(C) 그녀도 장미를 좋아해.
(D) 그게 더 낫다.

풀이 소녀의 튤립을 더 좋아한다는 말에 적절한 대답은 (A)이다.

Part C. Listen and Retell (p.39)

11. Girl: I can't spell "mother".
Boy: I'll ask the teacher to help you.
Question: How will the teacher help?
(D)

해석 소녀: 나는 "mother"을 쓸 수 없어.
소년: 너를 도울 수 있도록 선생님께 내가 여쭤볼게.
질문: 선생님이 어떻게 도와줄 것입니까?

풀이 소년이 mother을 쓸 줄 모르는 소녀를 돕기위해 선생님께 여쭙겠다고 했으므로 답은 (D)이다.

12. Boy: Why are you crying?
Girl: My stomach hurts.
Question: Which picture shows the girl?
(C)

해석 소년: 왜 울고 있어?
소녀: 배가 아파.
질문: 소녀를 묘사하는 그림은 무엇입니까?

풀이 소녀는 배가 아프다고 했으므로 답은 (C)이다.

Words and Phrases stomach (사람의) 위, 배

13. Girl: How much are the grapes?
Boy: They are 3 dollars.
Question: What is three dollars?
(A)

해석 소녀: 포도가 얼마에요?
소년: 3달러에요.
질문: 어떤 것이 3달러입니까?

풀이 포도가 3달러라고 했으므로 답은 (A)이다.

14. Boy: Do you like ice cream?
Girl: Yes, strawberry is my favorite.
Question: What's the girl's favorite ice cream?
(A) strawberry
(B) chocolate
(C) vanilla
(D) orange

해석 소년: 아이스크림을 좋아하니?
소녀: 응, 딸기를 가장 좋아해.
질문: 소녀가 가장 좋아하는 아이스크림은 무엇입니까?
(A) 딸기
(B) 초콜릿
(C) 바닐라
(D) 오렌지

풀이 소녀는 딸기 아이스크림을 가장 좋아한다고 했으므로 답은 (A)이다.

Words and Phrases favorite 가장 좋아하는

15. Boy: I like to sing songs.
Girl: Not me! I like to play video games.
Question: What does the girl like to do?
(A) listen to songs
(B) sing songs
(C) play songs
(D) play video games

해석 소년: 나는 노래 부르는 것을 좋아해.
소녀: 나는 아니야! 나는 비디오 게임을 하는 것을 좋아해.
질문: 소녀가 좋아하는 것은 무엇입니까?
(A) 노래를 듣다
(B) 노래를 부르다
(C) 노래를 연주하다
(D) 비디오 게임 하다

풀이 소녀는 비디오 게임 하는 것을 좋아한다고 했으므로 답은 (D)이다.

16. Boy: What would you like?
Girl: A pizza and a coke, please.
Question: Where are they?
(A) in a park
(B) at school
(C) in a bedroom
(D) in a restaurant

해석 소년: 무엇을 드시겠습니까?
소녀: 피자랑 콜라 부탁합니다.
질문: 그들은 어디에 있습니까?
(A) 공원에
(B) 학교에
(C) 침실에

(D) 레스토랑에

풀이 대화를 통해 소녀가 주문을 하는 상황임을 알 수 있으므로 답은 (D)이다.

17. Boy: How many brothers and sisters do you have?
Girl: I have five brothers. I don't have any sisters.
Question: How many sisters does the girl have?

(A) zero
(B) one
(C) two
(D) five

해석 소년: 너는 형제자매가 몇 명 있니?
소녀: 나는 형제가 5명이고, 자매는 없어.
질문: 소녀는 자매가 몇 명 있습니까?

(A) 0
(B) 1
(C) 2
(D) 5

풀이 소녀가 남자 형제는 5명이고, 자매는 없다고 했으므로 답은 (A)이다.

[18–19]

Girl: Joe loves to take baths. He fills the bath tub with lots of bubbles. He has a toy duck named "Quack" that he plays with. Quack is yellow and has blue eyes. Sometimes, Joe stays in the tub for too long. After 15 minutes, his mother always tells him to get out and dry off.

18. What does Joe love to do?

(A) take a bath
(B) blow bubbles
(C) feed the ducks
(D) talk with his mother

19. What is "Quack"?

(A) a bath tub
(B) a toy duck
(C) Joe's nickname
(D) a bubble machine

해석 소녀: Joe는 목욕하는 것을 좋아한다. 그는 욕조를 많은 거품으로 채운다. 그는 그가 가지고 노는 "Quack"이라 불리는 장난감 오리가 있다. Quack은 노란색이고 푸른 눈을 가지고 있다. 가끔, Joe는 욕조에 너무 오래 있는다. 15분 후 그의 엄마는 나가서 말리라고 항상 말한다.

18. Joe가 좋아하는 것은 무엇입니까?

(A) 목욕하다
(B) 거품을 불다
(C) 오리에게 먹이를 주다
(D) 엄마와 대화하다

19. Quack은 무엇입니까?

(A) 욕조
(B) 장난감 오리
(C) Joe의 별명
(D) 거품 기계

풀이 Joe는 목욕하는 것을 좋아하므로 18번의 답은 (A)이다. Quack은 Joe의 장난감 오리라고 했으므로 19번의 답은 (B)이다.

Words and Phrases fill 채우다 bubble 거품 dry off 말리다

[20–21]

Boy: Dogs are my favorite animals. I like them because they can run fast and love to catch balls. I take my dog to the park, and we play catch all day. He gets very happy and licks me in the face. I don't mind though because he's my best friend.

20. What does the boy like to throw for his dog?

(A) sticks
(B) balls
(C) pencils
(D) toys

21. What does the dog love to do?

(A) bite shoes
(B) eat sausages
(C) catch balls
(D) take a walk

해석 소년: 개는 내가 가장 좋아하는 동물이다. 나는 그들이 빨리 달릴 수 있고 캐치볼 하는 것을 좋아해서 그들을 좋아한다. 나는 나의 개를 공원으로 데려가고, 하루 종일 캐치볼을 한다. 그는 매우 행복해지고 내 얼굴을 핥는다. 그는 나의 가장 친한 친구이기 때문에 나는 꺼리지 않는다.

20. 소년은 그의 개를 위해 무엇을 던지는 것을 좋아합니까?

(A) 막대기
(B) 공
(C) 연필
(D) 장난감

21. 개는 무엇을 하는 것을 매우 좋아합니까?

(A) 신발 물다
(B) 소시지를 먹다
(C) 공을 잡다
(D) 산책하다

풀이 소년은 캐치볼을 한다고 했으므로 20번의 답은 (B)이다. 개는 캐치볼 하는 것을 좋아한다고 했으므로 21번의 답은 (C)이다.

[22–23]

Girl: Today is Wednesday, but I woke up late. My mom didn't wake me up because it's snowing, and school is cancelled. After lunch, I will call my friends to play outside. I want to make a snowman and have a snowball fight.

22. What's the weather like?

(A) sunny
(B) windy
(C) snowy
(D) rainy

23. What will the girl NOT do?

(A) make snowmen

(B) have a snowball fight

(C) play with friends

(D) go to school

해석 소녀: 오늘은 수요일이지만 나는 늦게 일어났다. 오늘 눈이 와서 학교가 취소되었기 때문에 엄마는 나를 깨우지 않았다. 점심 식사 후, 나는 밖에서 놀자고 친구들에게 전화를 할 것이다. 나는 눈사람을 만들고 눈싸움을 하고 싶다.

22. 날씨가 어떻습니까?

(A) 화창한

(B) 바람이 부는

(C) 눈이 오는

(D) 비가 오는

23. 소녀는 무엇을 하지 않을 것입니까?

(A) 눈사람 만들다

(B) 눈싸움을 하다

(C) 친구들과 놀다

(D) 학교에 가다

풀이 눈이 와서 학교가 취소되었다고 했으므로 22번의 답은 (C)이다. 학교가 취소되었다고 했으므로 23번의 답은 (D)이다.

Words and Phrases cancel 취소하다 snowball fight 눈싸움

[24–25]

Boy: The red panda lives in China and other parts of Asia. It is a little bigger than a cat and has a long, fluffy tail. Like giant pandas, red pandas eat a lot of bamboo. They like to live in trees. Sadly, there are not many red pandas left in the world.

24. How big is a red panda?

(A) smaller than a dog

(B) bigger than a cat

(C) bigger than a tree

(D) smaller than a bamboo tree

25. What is NOT true about red pandas?

(A) They live in trees.

(B) You can find them in China.

(C) They eat a lot of bamboo.

(D) They do not have a tail.

해석 소년: 너구리 판다는 중국과 아시아 다른 지역에서 산다. 이것은 고양이보다 조금 크고 길고 털이 많은 꼬리를 가지고 있다. 대왕 판다처럼, 너구리 판다는 대나무를 많이 먹는다. 그들은 나무 안에 사는 것을 좋아한다. 슬프게도 세계에는 너구리 판다가 많이 남아 있지 있다.

24. 너구리 판다는 얼마나 큽니까?

(A) 개보다 작다

(B) 고양이보다 크다

(C) 나무보다 크다

(D) 대나무보다 작다

25. 너구리 판다에 대한 사실이 아닌 것은 무엇입니까?

(A) 그들은 나무에 산다.

(B) 중국에서 발견할 수 있다.

(C) 많은 대나무를 먹는다.

(D) 꼬리가 없다.

풀이 너구리 판다는 고양이보다 크다고 했으므로 24번의 답은 (B)다. 털이 많은 꼬리를 가지고 있다고 했으므로 25번의 답은 (D)이다.

Words and Phrases red panda 너구리 판다 giant panda 대왕 판다 bamboo 대나무 fluffy 솜털로 뒤덮인

Part D. Listen and Speak (p.43)

26. Girl: Your pizza looks yummy.
Man: Would you like some?
Girl: Thanks. Would you like some of my fries?
Man: ____________________

(A) I don't like pizza.

(B) Is there candy?

(C) It's not hot.

(D) Thanks, I'd love some.

해석 소녀: 네 피자 맛있어 보인다.
남자: 좀 먹을래?
소녀: 고마워. 감자튀김 먹을래?
남자: ____________________

(A) 나는 피자를 싫어해.

(B) 사탕 있어?

(C) 뜨겁지 않아.

(D) 고마워, 조금 먹을래.

풀이 감자튀김을 먹을지 물었으므로 적절한 반응은 (D)이다.

27. Boy: I like animals.
Girl: What's your favorite animal?
Boy: I like horses the best.
Girl: ____________________

(A) They are very sweet.

(B) I like horses too!

(C) I like hamburgers.

(D) They listen to music.

해석 소년: 나는 동물을 좋아해.
소녀: 너가 가장 좋아하는 동물은 뭐니?
소년: 나는 말을 가장 좋아해.
소녀: ____________________

(A) 그들은 달콤해.

(B) 나도 말을 좋아해!

(C) 나는 햄버거가 좋아.

(D) 그들은 음악을 들어.

풀이 말을 가장 좋아한다는 소년의 말에 가장 적절한 반응은 (B)이다.

28. Girl: Who is she?
Boy: She's my teacher.
Girl: What's her name?
Boy: ____________________

(A) My name is James.
(B) His name is Mr. Jones.
(C) Her name is Ms. Jones.
(D) She's a teacher.

해석 소녀: 그녀는 누구야?
소년: 그녀는 내 선생님이야.
소녀: 그녀의 이름은 무엇이니?
소년: ______________
(A) 내 이름은 James야.
(B) 그의 이름은 Mr.Jones야.
(C) 그녀의 이름은 Ms.Jones야.
(D) 그녀는 선생님이야.

풀이 그녀의 이름을 물었으므로 답은 (C)이다. (B)는 남자 이름을 말한 것이므로 적절하지 않다.

29. Boy: Is it an animal?
Girl: No, it isn't.
Boy: Is it a flower?
Girl: ______________.
(A) No, I don't like flowers.
(B) No, it isn't.
(C) Yes, it's an animal.
(D) Yes, I like animals.

해석 소년: 그건 동물이야?
소녀: 아니야.
소년: 그건 꽃이야?
소녀: ______________
(A) 아니, 나는 꽃을 좋아하지 않아.
(B) 아니야.
(C) 응, 그것은 동물이야.
(D) 응, 나는 동물을 좋아해.

풀이 꽃인지 물었으므로 적절한 대답은 (B)이다.

30. Boy: Hi. Is Kenny home?
Girl: Yes, he is.
Boy: Can I talk to him please?
Girl: ______________
(A) Yes, you will.
(B) No, he isn't.
(C) OK, he is.
(D) Yes, you can.

해석 소년: 안녕. Kenny 집에 있어?
소녀: 응, 있어.
소년: 그와 통화할 수 있을까?
소녀: ______________
(A) 응, 넌 할거야.
(B) 아니, 그는 아니야.
(C) 그래, 그는 맞아.
(D) 응, 너는 할 수 있어.

풀이 Kenny와 통화할 수 있는지 물었으므로 답은 (D)이다.

SECTION II READING AND WRITING

Part A. Sentence Completion (p.46)

1. A: ______________ is he?
B: He's in his classroom.
(A) Who
(B) What
(C) Where
(D) Why

해석 A: 그는 **어디에** 있어?
B: 그는 교실에 있어.
(A) 누구
(B) 무엇
(C) 어디
(D) 왜

풀이 B가 위치로 대답한 것을 보아 A는 그가 어디에 있는지 물었음을 알 수 있다. 따라서 답은 (C)이다.

2. A: What does your father ______________?
B: He is a pilot.
(A) do
(B) did
(C) does
(D) doing

해석 A: 너의 아버지는 무엇을 **하시니**?
B: 그는 조종사이셔.
(A) 하다
(B) 했다
(C) 하다(3인칭 단수)
(D) 하는

풀이 '의문사 + do + 주어 + 동사원형' 형태로 빈칸에 동사원형이 들어가야 한다. 따라서 답은 (A)이다.

Words and Phrases pilot 비행기 조종사

3. A: Can you help me ______________ the car?
B: Sure. Pass the soap.
(A) wash
(B) washes
(C) washed
(D) washing

해석 A: 내가 차 **닦는** 것을 도와줄 수 있니?
B: 당연하지. 비누 줘.
(A) 닦다
(B) 닦다(3인칭 단수)
(C) 닦았다
(D) 닦는

풀이 'help + 목적어' 뒤에 동사원형 또는 to + 동사원형이 올 수 있다. 따라서 답은 (A)이다.

Words and Phrases pass 건네주다, 지나가다

4. A: How old are ______________ friends?
B: They are 11 years old.
(A) you
(B) your
(C) mine
(D) yours

해석 A: **네** 친구들은 몇 살이니?
B: 그들은 11살이야.
(A) 너
(B) 너의
(C) 내 것
(D) 너의 것

풀이 A는 B의 친구들 나이에 대해 물어보고 있으므로 '너의'라는 뜻의 'your'가 빈칸에 와야 한다. 따라서 답은 (B)이다.

5. A: What does she do __________ Mondays?
B: She goes to ballet class.
(A) in
(B) on
(C) at
(D) over

해석 A: 그녀는 월요일**에** 무엇을 하니?
B: 그녀는 발레 수업을 가.
(A) ~에
(B) ~에
(C) ~에
(D) ~위에

풀이 요일 앞에 전치사 'on'을 사용하므로 답은 (B)이다. 'in'은 월, 연도, 계절 앞에 쓰이며 'at'은 특정 시간 앞에 쓰인다.

Part B. Situational Writing (p.47)

6. The rabbit is __________________.
(A) jumping
(B) sleeping
(C) eating
(D) playing

해석 토끼는 **자고 있다**.
(A) 점프하다
(B) 자다
(C) 먹다
(D) 놀다

풀이 그림의 토끼는 자고 있으므로 답은 (B)이다.

7. My __________________ is very old.
(A) uncle
(B) father
(C) grandfather
(D) grandmother

해석 나의 **할머니**는 나이가 매우 많다.
(A) 삼촌
(B) 아빠
(C) 할아버지
(D) 할머니

풀이 그림에는 나이 많은 여자 노인이 있으므로 답은 (D)이다.

8. The girl is putting cream on his __________________.
(A) chin
(B) nose
(C) hand
(D) cheek

해석 소녀는 소년의 **뺨**에 크림을 묻히고 있다.
(A) 턱
(B) 코
(C) 손
(D) 뺨

풀이 소녀가 소년의 뺨에 크림을 묻히고 있으므로 답은 (D)이다.
Words and Phrases chin 턱 cheek 볼, 뺨

9. The kids are __________________.
(A) in the park
(B) in the tree
(C) on the bench
(D) in the pond

해석 아이들은 **공원에** 있다.
(A) 공원에
(B) 나무에
(C) 벤치 위에
(D) 연못 안에

풀이 그림에서 아이들이 공원에서 놀고 있으므로 답은 (A)이다.

10. The woman is __________________.
(A) feeding the dog
(B) talking to her friend
(C) short and blonde
(D) wearing glasses

해석 여자는 **안경을 쓰고 있다**.
(A) 개에게 밥을 주다
(B) 친구와 대화하다
(C) 작고 금발이다
(D) 안경을 쓰다

풀이 그림의 여자는 안경을 쓰고 있으므로 답은 (D)이다.
Words and Phrases blonde 금발

Part C. Practical Reading and Retelling (p.49)

[11–12]

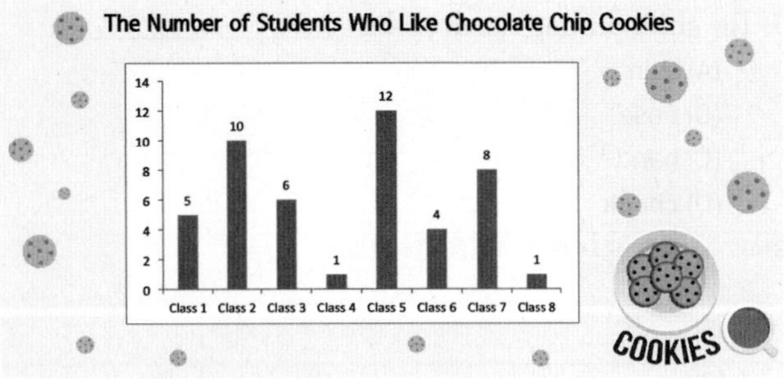

11. How many students in Class 3 like chocolate chip cookies?
   (A) 4
   (B) 6
   (C) 10
   (D) 12

12. Which class likes chocolate chip cookies the most?
   (A) Class 1
   (B) Class 3
   (C) Class 5
   (D) Class 7

해석 11. 3반에서 초콜릿 칩 쿠키를 좋아하는 학생은 몇 명입니까?
   (A) 4
   (B) 6
   (C) 10
   (D) 12

12. 초콜릿 칩 쿠키를 가장 좋아하는 반은 몇 반입니까?
   (A) 1반
   (B) 3반
   (C) 5반
   (D) 7반

풀이 3반은 6명이 좋아하므로 11번의 답은 (B)이다. 5반의 총 12명이 초콜릿 칩 쿠키를 좋아하므로 그 수가 가장 많다. 따라서 12번의 답은 (C)이다.

[13–14]

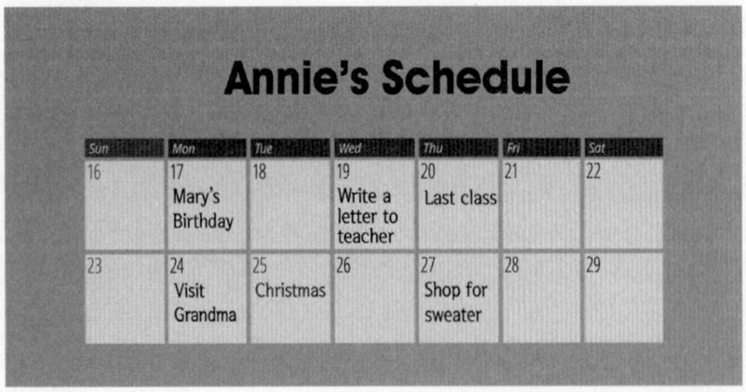

13. What month is it?
   (A) January
   (B) March
   (C) August
   (D) December

14. When does Annie visit grandma?
   (A) on the 17th
   (B) on the 19th
   (C) on the 24th
   (D) on the 27th

해석 13. 어느 달입니까?
   (A) 1월
   (B) 3월
   (C) 8월
   (D) 12월

14. Annie는 언제 할머니 댁을 방문합니까?
   (A) 17일에
   (B) 19일에
   (C) 24일에
   (D) 27일에

풀이 크리스마스가 있는 것으로 보아 12월이므로 13번의 답은 (D)이다. 할머니 댁을 방문하는 날은 24일이므로 14번의 답은 (C)이다.

Words and Phrases schedule 시간표, 일정표 sweater 스웨터

[15–16]

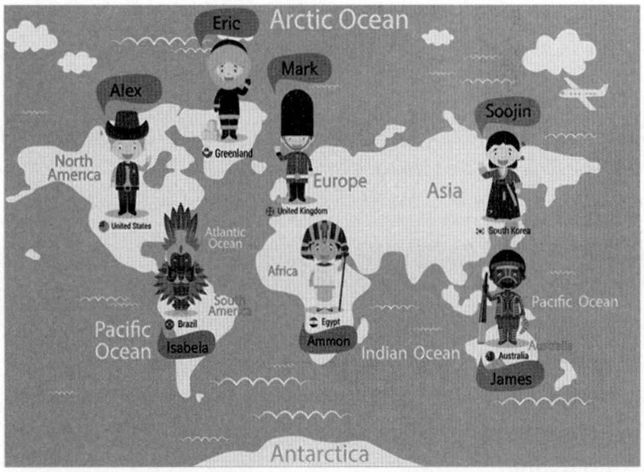

15. Where does Alex live?
   (A) in Korea
   (B) in America
   (C) in England
   (D) in Africa

16. Who lives in Asia?
   (A) Eric
   (B) Soojin
   (C) Isabela
   (D) Mark

해석 15. Alex는 어디에 삽니까?
   (A) 한국에
   (B) 미국에
   (C) 영국에

(D) 아프리카에

16. 아시아에 사는 사람은 누구입니까?
(A) Eric
(B) Soojin
(C) Isabela
(D) Mark

풀이 Alex는 미국에 사므로 15번의 답은 (B)이다. 아시아에 포함 되는 것은 Soojin이 사는 한국이므로 16번의 답은 (B)이다.

Words and Phrases Greenland 그린란드 Arctic Ocean 북극해
Pacific Ocean 태평양

[17–18]

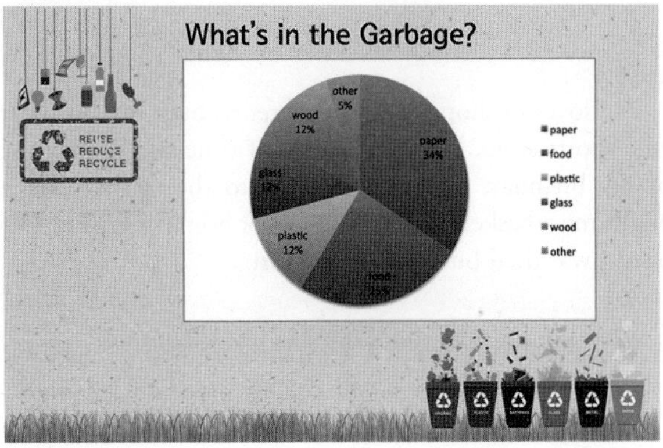

17. What makes the most garbage?
(A) food
(B) plastic
(C) paper
(D) glass

18. Which three are the same percentage?
(A) food, plastic, and glass
(B) plastic, glass, and wood
(C) glass, wood, and other
(D) food, paper, and other

해석 17. 가장 많은 쓰레기를 만드는 것은 무엇입니까?
(A) 음식물
(B) 플라스틱
(C) 종이
(D) 유리

18. 같은 퍼센트를 차지하는 세 가지는 무엇입니까?
(A) 음식, 플라스틱, 유리
(B) 플라스틱, 유리, 나무
(C) 유리, 나무, 기타
(D) 음식, 종이, 기타

풀이 종이가 34%로 가장 많으므로 17번의 답은 (C)이다. 플라스틱, 유리, 나무 모두 12%이므로 18번의 답은 (B)이다.

Words and Phrases garbage 쓰레기 percentage 백분율, 비율

[19–20]

19. Where is the clock?
(A) in the bedroom
(B) in the kitchen
(C) in the living room
(D) in the study room

20. Where is the bedroom?
(A) on the balcony
(B) between the bathroom and study room
(C) next to the living room
(D) between the living room and the kitchen

해석 19. 시계는 어디에 있습니까?
(A) 침실에
(B) 부엌에
(C) 거실에
(D) 공부방에

20. 침실은 어디에 있습니까?
(A) 발코니에
(B) 화장실과 공부방 사이에
(C) 거실 옆에
(D) 거실과 부엌 사이에

풀이 시계는 거실에 있으므로 19번의 답은 (C)이다. 그림에서 침실은 2층의 욕실과 공부방 사이에 있으므로 20번의 답은 (B)이다.

Part D. General Reading and Retelling (p.54)

[21–22]
Skiing is one of my favorite winter sports. Every winter, I go with my father and climb up the snowy hills. We do not ski very fast, but it is still fun. Even if I fall, it does not hurt because the snow is so soft.

21. What does the writer like to do in the winter?
(A) make snowmen
(B) play chess
(C) run on mountains

(D) ski on hills

22. According to the passage, which sentence is true?

(A) They ski on tall mountains.

(B) The writer skis alone.

(C) It does not hurt when the writer falls.

(D) The writer does not have fun when they skis.

해석 스키 타는 것은 내가 가장 좋아하는 겨울 스포츠 중 하나이다. 매 겨울, 나는 아빠와 가서 눈 덮인 언덕을 등반한다. 우리는 스키를 매우 빨리 타지는 않지만, 그것은 여전히 재미있다. 내가 넘어지더라도, 눈이 너무 부드러워서 아프지 않다.

21. 글쓴이는 겨울에 무엇을 하는 것을 좋아합니까?

(A) 눈사람을 만들다

(B) 체스를 하다

(C) 산에서 뛰다

(D) 언덕에서 스키를 타다

22. 지문에 따르면, 사실인 것은 무엇입니까?

(A) 그들은 높은 산에서 스키를 탄다.

(B) 글쓴이는 혼자 스키를 탄다.

(C) 글쓴이는 넘어질 때 아프지 않다.

(D) 글쓴이는 그들이 스키를 탈 때 재미를 못 느낀다.

풀이 글쓴이는 눈 덮인 언덕에 올라가 스키 타는 것을 좋아한다고 했으므로 21번의 답은 (D)이다. 눈이 부드러워서 넘어져도 안 아프다고 했으므로 22번의 답은 (C)이다.

Words and Phrases climb 오르다, 올라가다 chess 체스, 장기

[23–24]

My friend Lisa has the perfect hobby. She collects buttons. She has over one hundred different buttons. She finds buttons everywhere. She finds them in the park, under sofas, and even at school. Sometimes she buys them at the sewing shop. She loves all buttons, but her favorite ones are purple.

23. How many buttons does Lisa have?

(A) less than ten

(B) just fifty

(C) over one hundred

(D) over one thousand

24. What color are her favorites?

(A) white

(B) purple

(C) green

(D) red

해석 내 친구 Lisa는 완벽한 취미를 가지고 있다. 그녀는 단추를 모은다. 그녀는 100개가 넘는 다른 단추를 가지고 있다. 그녀는 모든 곳에서 단추를 찾는다. 그녀는 공원에서, 소파 아래서, 그리고 심지어 학교에서도 찾는다. 가끔 그녀는 바느질 가게에서 단추를 산다. 그녀는 모든 단추를 좋아하지만 그녀가 가장 좋아하는 것은 보라색이다.

23. Lisa는 단추를 몇 개 가지고 있습니까?

(A) 10개 미만

(B) 50개

(C) 100개 초과

(D) 1000개 초과

24. 그녀가 가장 좋아하는 것은 어떤 색깔입니까?

(A) 흰색

(B) 보라색

(C) 초록색

(D) 빨간색

풀이 Lisa는 100개가 넘는 단추를 가지고 있다고 했으므로 23번의 답은 (C)이다.
Lisa는 보라색을 가장 좋아한다고 했으므로 24번의 답은 (B)이다.

Words and Phrases button 단추 sewing shop 바느질 가게
perfect 완벽한

[25–26]

My dad loves to shop at many different stores, but his favorite is the sports store. He spends a lot of time and money there. For my birthday, my dad took me to the sports store and bought me a basketball. We went back home and played for 3 hours! I was tired but had a lot of fun.

25. What kind of store does the dad like the most?

(A) grocery store

(B) clothes store

(C) shoes store

(D) sports store

26. What did the writer get for his birthday?

(A) a basketball

(B) a baseball

(C) a tennis ball

(D) a soccer ball

해석 아빠는 많은 다른 가게에서 쇼핑하는 것을 좋아하지만, 그가 가장 좋아하는 것은 운동 용품 가게이다. 그는 거기에 많은 시간과 돈을 쏟는다. 내 생일을 위해서, 아빠는 운동 용품 가게로 나를 데려가서 농구공을 사주셨다. 우리는 집으로 돌아가서 3시간 동안 운동했다! 나는 피곤했지만 매우 재미있었다.

25. 아빠는 어떤 종류의 가게를 가장 좋아합니까?

(A) 식료품점

(B) 옷 가게

(C) 신발 가게

(D) 운동 용품 가게

26. 작가는 그의 생일에 무엇을 받았습니까?

(A) 농구공

(B) 야구공

(C) 테니스공

(D) 축구공

풀이 아빠는 운동 용품 가게를 가장 좋아한다고 했으므로 25번의 답은 (D)이다. 작가는 농구공을 받았으므로 26번의 답은 (A)이다.

Words and Phrases grocery store 식품점, 슈퍼마켓

[27–28]
Mice are small animals. Most are gray or brown. They live in the grass and sometimes in the walls of people's homes. People are scared of mice, but they are not usually dangerous. Many people think mice like cheese, but they actually like sweet food more. It is easier to catch a mouse with sweets than with cheese.

27. What color are most mice?
(A) black only
(B) gray only
(C) gray or brown
(D) brown and black

28. What do mice like to do?
(A) hurt and scare people
(B) swim in the water
(C) play with small animals
(D) eat sweet food

해석 쥐는 작은 동물이다. 대부분은 회색이나 갈색이다. 그들은 풀에서 살고 가끔 사람들 집의 벽에서 산다. 사람들은 쥐를 무서워하지만 그들은 주로 위험하지 않다. 많은 사람들은 쥐가 치즈를 좋아한다고 생각하지만, 그들은 사실 단 음식을 더 좋아한다. 치즈보다 단 것으로 쥐를 잡는 것이 더 쉽다.

27. 대부분의 쥐는 무슨 색입니까?
(A) 오직 검정색
(B) 오직 회색
(C) 회색 혹은 갈색
(D) 갈색과 검정색

28. 쥐들은 무엇을 하는 것을 좋아합니까?
(A) 사람들을 다치게 하거나 겁먹게 하다
(B) 물에서 수영하다
(C) 작은 동물들과 놀다
(D) 단 음식을 먹다

풀이 쥐는 대부분 회색이나 갈색이라고 했으므로 27번의 답은 (C)이다. 쥐는 단 음식을 먹는 것을 좋아한다고 했으므로 28번의 답은 (D)이다.
Words and Phrases dangerous 위험한

[29–30]
Tom is a good baseball player. He is very strong and can hit the ball a long way. This year he hit 10 homeruns! He runs fast and is good at catching the ball. He is always kind to other players as well. This year he was chosen as the team MVP.

29. What does Tom NOT do?
(A) kick the ball
(B) catch the ball
(C) hit the ball
(D) run very fast

30. What kind of player is Tom?
(A) a slow runner
(B) a bad catcher
(C) a good hitter
(D) a good dancer

해석 Tom은 좋은 야구 선수다. 그는 힘이 매우 세고 공을 멀리 칠 수 있다. 올해 그는 10개의 홈런을 쳤다! 그는 빨리 달리고 공을 잘 잡는다. 그는 또한 항상 다른 선수들에게 친절하다. 올해 그는 팀의 MVP로 선정되었다.

29. Tom이 하지 않는 것은 무엇입니까?
(A) 공을 차다
(B) 공을 잡다
(C) 공을 치다
(D) 매우 빨리 달리다

30. Tom은 어떤 종류의 선수입니까?
(A) 느리게 달리는 사람
(B) 잘 못 잡는 사람
(C) 잘 치는 사람
(D) 춤을 잘 추는 사람

풀이 지문에서 Tom은 공을 멀리 치고, 빨리 달리고, 공을 잘 잡는다고 했다. 공을 찬다는 내용은 없으므로, 29번의 답은 (A) 이다. Tom은 공을 멀리 칠 수 있고, 올해 10개의 홈런까지 쳤다고 했으므로 30번의 답은 (C)이다.
Words and Phrases catcher (야구) 포수 hitter (야구) 타자

TOSEL BASIC

실전 3회

Section I Listening and Speaking

1 **(B)**	2 **(A)**	3 **(C)**	4 **(D)**	5 **(C)**
6 **(C)**	7 **(D)**	8 **(B)**	9 **(D)**	10 **(D)**
11 **(A)**	12 **(D)**	13 **(A)**	14 **(B)**	15 **(C)**
16 **(B)**	17 **(D)**	18 **(A)**	19 **(C)**	20 **(B)**
21 **(C)**	22 **(A)**	23 **(B)**	24 **(B)**	25 **(C)**
26 **(A)**	27 **(B)**	28 **(C)**	29 **(A)**	30 **(A)**

Section II Reading and Writing

1 **(C)**	2 **(A)**	3 **(A)**	4 **(C)**	5 **(C)**
6 **(D)**	7 **(C)**	8 **(B)**	9 **(D)**	10 **(B)**
11 **(B)**	12 **(B)**	13 **(B)**	14 **(D)**	15 **(D)**
16 **(A)**	17 **(A)**	18 **(B)**	19 **(B)**	20 **(C)**
21 **(A)**	22 **(D)**	23 **(A)**	24 **(C)**	25 **(C)**
26 **(C)**	27 **(B)**	28 **(A)**	29 **(D)**	30 **(B)**

SECTION I LISTENING AND SPEAKING

Part A. Listen and Recognize (p.61)

1. Girl: Today, it is sunny and sometimes cloudy.
   (B)

해석 소녀: 오늘은 맑고 가끔 구름이 끼겠습니다.
풀이 맑고 구름이 낀다고 했으므로 답은 (B)이다.

2. Girl: I have some green apples.
   (A)

해석 소녀: 나는 초록색 사과를 몇 개 가지고 있다.
풀이 초록색 사과를 가지고 있다고 했으므로 답은 (A)이다.

3. Boy: There is a television on the table.
   (C)

해석 소년: 탁자 위에 텔레비전이 있다.
풀이 탁자 위에 텔레비전이 있는 그림 (C)가 답이다.

4. Girl: The boy doesn't like pizza.
   (D)

해석 소녀: 소년은 피자를 좋아하지 않는다.
풀이 피자를 먹고 싶어하지 않는 그림 (D)가 답이다.

5. Boy: They're riding bikes.
   (C)

해석 소년: 그들은 자전거를 타고 있다.
풀이 자전거를 타고 있는 사람들 그림 (C)가 답이다.

PART B. Listen and Respond (p.63)

6. Girl: Do you want to watch a movie?
   Boy: ____________________
   (A) No, he went to school.
   (B) I'm hungry.
   (C) Yes, let's go now.
   (D) I'm a student.

해석 소녀: 영화 볼래?
소년: ______________
(A) 아니, 그는 학교에 갔어.
(B) 나는 배가 고파.
(C) 응, 지금 가자.
(D) 나는 학생이야.
풀이 영화를 보자는 소녀의 제안에 가장 적절한 대답은 (C)이다.

7. Boy: How many students are in your class?
   Girl: ____________________
   (A) No, we went to school together.
   (B) Yes, they do.
   (C) I'm ten years old.
   (D) There are fifteen.

해석 소년: 너네 반에 학생이 몇 명 있어?
소녀: ______________
(A) 아니, 우리는 학교에 같이 갔어.
(B) 응, 그들은 해.
(C) 나는 10살이야.
(D) 15명이 있어.
풀이 학생이 몇 명 있는지 물어보았으므로 숫자로 답한 (D)가 정답이다.

8. Girl: Why are you smiling?
   Boy: ____________________
   (A) I have a headache.
   (B) I won a prize.
   (C) I lost my pen.
   (D) My friends don't like me.

해석 소녀: 왜 웃고 있니?
소년: ______________
(A) 나는 머리가 아파.
(B) 상을 탔어.
(C) 내 펜을 잃어버렸어.
(D) 내 친구들이 나를 좋아하지 않아.
풀이 웃고 있는 적절한 이유로 보기 중 가장 적절한 것은 (B)이다.

9. Boy: I brought your hat.
   Girl: ____________________
   (A) I like hats.
   (B) Where is he?

(C) Is there a bag?

(D) Thank you very much.

해석 소년: 너의 모자를 가져왔어.

소녀: ________________

(A) 나는 모자를 좋아해.

(B) 그는 어디에 있니?

(C) 가방이 있어?

(D) 정말 고마워.

풀이 소녀의 모자를 가지고 왔다는 소년의 말에 적절한 반응은 (D)이다.

10. Boy: Where is your textbook?
Girl: ________________

(A) It's mine now.

(B) It's new to me.

(C) It's bigger than before.

(D) It's on the table.

해석 소년: 네 교과서 어디 있어?

소녀: ________________

(A) 이제 내 거야.

(B) 나에게 새로워.

(C) 전보다 크다.

(D) 테이블 위에 있어.

풀이 교과서의 위치를 물었으므로 장소로 답한 (D)가 답이다.

Part C. Listen and Retell (p.64)

11. Boy: Excuse me, is there a flower shop near here?
Girl: It's next to the hospital.
Question: Where is the flower shop?

(A)

해석 소년: 실례합니다, 여기 근처에 꽃집이 있나요?

소녀: 병원 옆에 있어요.

질문: 꽃집은 어디에 있습니까?

풀이 꽃집은 병원 옆에 있다고 했으므로 답은 (A)이다.

12. Girl: I'm hungry. Do you have any cookies?
Boy: They're on the table. Help yourself.
Question: What does the girl want to have?

(D)

해석 소녀: 난 배가 고파. 쿠키 있어?

소년: 테이블 위에 있어. 마음껏 먹어.

질문: 소녀는 무엇을 먹고 싶어 합니까?

풀이 소녀가 쿠키가 있냐고 물었으므로 답은 (D)이다.

Words and Phrases help yourself 마음껏 먹어

13. Boy: What are you doing after school?
Girl: I'm going to play basketball. Do you want to join?
Question: What are they doing after school?

(A)

해석 소년: 방과 후에 뭐해?

소녀: 나는 농구를 할 거야. 너도 할래?

질문: 그들은 방과 후에 무엇을 합니까?

풀이 방과 후에 농구를 한다고 했으므로 답은 (A)이다.

14. Girl: How is your brother?
Boy: He plays on the soccer team now, so he's happy.
Question: Why is his brother happy?

(A) He studies hard.

(B) He plays soccer.

(C) He watches TV.

(D) He reads books.

해석 소녀: 네 남동생 잘 지내?

소년: 그는 지금 축구팀에서 경기해서 행복해.

질문: 왜 그의 남동생은 행복합니까?

(A) 그는 열심히 공부한다.

(B) 그는 축구를 한다.

(C) 그는 TV를 본다.

(D) 그는 책을 읽는다.

풀이 축구팀에서 경기해서 행복하다고 했으므로 답은 (B)이다.

15. Boy: Why does your mom always go to the hospital?
Girl: She works there. She helps people.
Question: What does the girl's mom probably do?

(A) She's a teacher.

(B) She's a pilot.

(C) She's a nurse.

(D) She's a firefighter.

해석 소년: 왜 너희 엄마는 항상 병원에 가시니?

소녀: 그녀는 거기서 일하셔. 사람들을 도우셔.

질문: 소녀의 어머니는 아마 어떤 일을 하십니까?

(A) 그녀는 선생님이다.

(B) 그녀는 비행기 조종사다.

(C) 그녀는 간호사다.

(D) 그녀는 소방관이다.

풀이 소녀가 병원에서 엄마가 일한다고 했으므로 보기 중 가장 적절한 답은 (C)이다.

16. Girl: Do you like music?
Boy: It's all right, but I prefer watching movies.
Question: What does the boy like?

(A) music

(B) movies

(C) soccer

(D) books

해석 소녀: 음악을 좋아하니?

소년: 괜찮은데, 나는 영화 보는 것을 더 좋아해.

질문: 소년은 무엇을 좋아합니까?

(A) 음악

(B) 영화

(C) 축구

(D) 책

풀이 소년은 영화보는 것을 더 좋아한다고 했으므로 답은 (B)이다.

17. Boy: Can I borrow your umbrella?

Girl: Sorry, it's raining, and I have to walk home.
Question: How is the weather?

(A) It's windy.
(B) It's cloudy.
(C) It's too hot.
(D) It's raining.

해석 소년: 네 우산을 빌려도 되니?
소녀: 미안해, 비가 와, 그리고 나는 집에 걸어 가야해.
질문: 날씨가 어떻습니까?
(A) 바람이 분다.
(B) 구름이 낀다.
(C) 너무 덥다.
(D) 비가 온다.

풀이 비가 온다고 했으므로 답은 (D)이다.

[18–19]

Girl: This afternoon I played with my cat. Her name is "Socks". I held a ball on a string, and Socks tried to grab it. When we finished playing, my mom gave her some food. She must have been hungry. She ate and then went to sleep.

18. What did the mom do?

(A) She gave the cat food.
(B) She put the cat outside.
(C) She put the cat to bed.
(D) She washed the cat.

19. What did the cat do after eating?

(A) play
(B) walk
(C) sleep
(D) eat

해석 소녀: 오늘 오후 나는 고양이와 놀았다. 그녀의 이름은 "Socks"이다. 나는 공이 매달린 끈을 들었고 Socks는 잡으려고 노력했다. 우리가 노는 것을 끝냈을 때, 엄마는 그녀에게 음식을 조금 주었다. 그녀는 배고팠음에 틀림없다. 그녀는 먹고나서 잠을 잤다.

18. 엄마는 무엇을 했습니까?
(A) 고양이에게 음식을 주었다.
(B) 고양이를 밖에 두었다.
(C) 고양이를 침대에 두었다.
(D) 고양이를 씻겼다.

19. 고양이는 먹고난 후 무엇을 했습니까?
(A) 놀다
(B) 걷다
(C) 자다
(D) 먹다

풀이 엄마는 고양이에게 음식을 주었다고 했으므로 18번의 답은 (A)이다. 고양이는 먹고 잠을 잤다고 했으므로 19번의 답은 (C)이다.

Words and Phrases string 끈, 줄 grab 붙잡다, 움켜잡다

[20–21]

Girl: Sally likes watching TV and reading books. Every Saturday and Sunday morning, she wakes up early to watch all of her favorite cartoons. On Saturdays, she goes with her brother to the library. There, she gets seven books: one to read every day of the week.

20. Who does Sally go to the library with?

(A) her mother
(B) her brother
(C) her father
(D) her sister

21. When does Sally watch cartoons?

(A) Monday and Tuesday
(B) Sunday and Monday
(C) Saturday and Sunday
(D) Friday and Saturday

해석 소녀: Sally는 TV를 보는 것과 책을 읽는 것을 좋아한다. 매주 토요일과 일요일 아침 그녀는 그녀가 좋아하는 만화를 모두 보기 위해 일찍 일어난다. 토요일에는, 남동생과 도서관에 간다. 그곳에서, 그녀는 7권의 책을 빌린다: 한 주 동안 하루에 하나씩 읽도록

20. Sally는 누구와 함께 도서관에 갑니까?
(A) 그녀의 엄마
(B) 그녀의 남동생
(C) 그녀의 아버지
(D) 그녀의 여동생

21. Sally는 언제 만화를 봅니까?
(A) 월요일과 화요일
(B) 일요일과 월요일
(C) 토요일과 일요일
(D) 금요일과 토요일

풀이 Sally는 남동생과 도서관에 간다고 했으므로 20번의 답은 (B)이다. Sally는 토요일과 일요일 아침에 만화를 본다고 했으므로 21번의 답은 (C)이다.

[22–23]

Boy: My sister is a teacher. She has many students, so she is very busy. Right now, she works as an English teacher, but she wants to teach Chinese, too. On the weekends, she studies Chinese during her free time. She is very smart, so I hope she reaches her goal.

22. What does his sister do?

(A) She's a teacher.
(B) She's a pilot.
(C) She's a doctor.
(D) She's a student.

23. What does she do on the weekends?

(A) study English

(B) study Chinese
(C) take a test
(D) travel to China

해석 소년: 나의 누나는 선생님이다. 그녀는 많은 학생들이 있어서 그녀는 매우 바쁘다. 현재, 그녀는 영어 선생님으로 일하지만 그녀는 또한 중국어를 가르치고 싶어한다. 주말에, 그녀는 그녀의 자유 시간에 중국어를 공부한다. 그녀는 매우 똑똑해서, 나는 그녀가 그녀의 목표에 도달했으면 좋겠다.

22. 그의 누나의 직업은 무엇입니까?
(A) 그녀는 선생님이다.
(B) 그녀는 비행기 조종사다.
(C) 그녀는 의사다.
(D) 그녀는 학생이다.

23. 그녀는 주말에 무엇을 합니까?
(A) 영어를 공부하다
(B) 중국어를 공부하다
(C) 시험을 보다
(D) 중국으로 여행가다

풀이 누나는 선생님이라고 했으므로 22번의 답은 (A)이다. 그녀는 주말 자유 시간에 중국어를 공부한다고 했으므로 23번의 답은 (B)이다.

[24–25]
Girl: Today is my friend Julie's birthday. She is turning nine years old. We are going to have her birthday party in the park. After we play some games, we will eat cake. Then, Julie will open her presents. I got her a doll. I hope she likes it!

24. How old will Julie be?
(A) eight years old
(B) nine years old
(C) ten years old
(D) eleven years old

25. Where is she going on her birthday?
(A) to the zoo
(B) to the library
(C) to the park
(D) to the swimming pool

해석 소녀: 오늘은 내 친구 Julie의 생일이다. 그녀는 9살이 된다. 우리는 공원에서 그녀의 생일 파티를 할 것이다. 우리가 게임을 조금 한 후, 우리는 케이크를 먹을 것이다. 그리고, Julie는 선물을 열 것이다. 나는 그녀에게 인형을 사 주었다. 그녀가 좋아했으면 좋겠다!

24. Julie는 몇 살이 될 것입니까?
(A) 8살
(B) 9살
(C) 10살
(D) 11살

25. 그녀는 생일에 어디에 갈 것입니까?
(A) 동물원에
(B) 도서관에
(C) 공원에
(D) 수영장에

풀이 Julie는 9살이 된다고 했으므로 24번의 답은 (B)이다. Julie의 생일파티는 공원에서 한다고 했으므로 25번의 답은 (C)이다.

Words and Phrases turn 나이가 ~가 되다 present 선물

Part D. Listen and Speak (p.68)

26. Boy: What did you do?
Girl: I had lunch.
Boy: What did you eat?
Girl: ____________________.
(A) A sandwich
(B) A ball
(C) An eraser
(D) A pot

해석 소년: 너는 무엇을 했니?
소녀: 점심을 먹었어.
소년: 무엇을 먹었어?
소녀: ____________________.
(A) 샌드위치
(B) 공
(C) 지우개
(D) 냄비

풀이 무엇을 먹었는지 물었으므로 먹을 수 있는 것으로 답한 (A)가 답이다.

Words and Phrases pot 냄비

27. Girl: Where is your school?
Boy: It's on Green Street.
Girl: My sister goes there, too!
Boy: ____________________
(A) It's green.
(B) Really?
(C) It's old.
(D) Where is your mom?

해석 소녀: 네 학교 어디에 있어?
소년: Green가에 있어.
소녀: 내 여동생도 거기 다녀!
소년: ____________________
(A) 초록색이야.
(B) 정말?
(C) 낡았어.
(D) 어머니 어디 계셔?

풀이 여동생이 같은 학교에 다닌다는 말에 적절한 반응은 (B)다.

28. Boy: I like your bag.
Girl: Thank you.
Boy: Is it new?
Girl: ____________________
(A) No, thanks.

(B) Yes, please.
(C) Yes, it is.
(D) No, he isn't.

해석 소년: 네 가방 마음에 들어.
소녀: 고마워.
소년: 새 거야?
소녀: ____________
(A) 아니, 괜찮아.
(B) 응, 해줘.
(C) 응, 맞아.
(D) 아니, 그는 아니야.

풀이 가방이 새것이냐고 물어보았으므로 그렇다고 대답한 (C)가 적절하다.

29. Girl: Hey. How are you?
Boy: I don't feel well today.
Girl: What's wrong?
Boy: ________________
(A) I have a headache.
(B) I have a hat.
(C) I have a drink.
(D) I have a book.

해석 소녀: 안녕. 잘 지내?
소년: 나는 오늘 몸이 안 좋아.
소녀: 무슨 일이야?
소년: ________________
(A) 나는 두통이 있어.
(B) 나는 모자가 있어.
(C) 나는 음료가 있어.
(D) 나는 책이 있어.

풀이 소년이 몸이 안 좋다고 했으므로 보기 중 가장 적절한 대답은 (A)가 답이다.

30. Boy: Why are you crying?
Girl: I can't find my money.
Boy: I can give you some money.
Girl: ________________
(A) Are you sure?
(B) Who is he?
(C) Where is the bank?
(D) No, I don't have any money.

해석 소년: 왜 울고 있니?
소녀: 나는 돈을 찾을 수가 없어.
소년: 내가 돈을 좀 줄 수 있어.
소녀: ____________
(A) 정말이야?
(B) 그는 누구야?
(C) 은행은 어디에 있어?
(D) 아니, 나는 돈이 없어.

풀이 돈을 줄 수 있다는 소년의 말을 확인하는 (A)가 가장 적절하다.

SECTION II READING AND WRITING

Part A. Sentence Completion (p.71)

1. A: How ____________ are you?
B: I'm nine years old.
(A) many
(B) much
(C) old
(D) time

해석 A: 너 몇 **살**이니?
B: 나는 9살이야.
(A) 많은
(B) 많은
(C) ~살 (how와 함께 쓰여 몇 살)
(D) 시간

풀이 how old는 몇 살인지 물어볼 때 쓰는 표현이므로 답은 (C)이다.

2. A: Where do you ____________?
B: In Seoul, Korea.
(A) live
(B) living
(C) to live
(D) are living

해석 A: 너 어디 **사니**?
B: 한국의 서울에.
(A) 살다
(B) 사는
(C) 살기 위한
(D) 살고 있는

풀이 '의문사 + do + 동사원형'의 형태로 빈칸에 동사원형이 와야 한다. 따라서 답은 (A)이다.

3. A: ____________ do you do on Saturdays?
B: I go to my grandmother's house.
(A) What
(B) When
(C) Why
(D) How

해석 A: 토요일에 **무엇**을 하니?
B: 할머니 댁에 가.
(A) 무엇
(B) 언제
(C) 왜
(D) 어떻게

풀이 동사 do와 함께 쓰였으므로 무엇을 하는지 묻는 것임을 알 수 있다. 따라서 답은 (A)이다.

4. A: Did you see the movie?
B: Yes, but I don't want to spoil the movie ____________ you see it.

(A) after

(B) when

(C) before

(D) because

해석 A: 너 그 영화 봤어?

B: 응, 하지만 네가 그것을 보기 **전에** 영화를 망치고 싶지 않아.

(A) ~후에

(B) ~(할) 때

(C) ~전에

(D) ~때문에

풀이 빈칸에는 시간 관계를 연결하면서 '~전에'라는 의미가 와야 한다. 따라서 답은 (C)이다.

5. A: How was the weather yesterday?
B: It was the __________!

(A) hot

(B) hotter

(C) hottest

(D) most hot

해석 A: 어제 날씨 어땠니?

B: **가장 더웠어!**

(A) 더운

(B) 더 더운

(C) 가장 더운

(D) 틀린 표현

풀이 정관사 the가 있는 것으로 보아 최상급이 와야 하므로 답은 (C)이다. (B)는 'hotter' 뒤에 'than + 비교대상'이 있으면 '~보다 더운'이라는 뜻이다.

Part B. Situational Writing (p.72)

6. I like going to __________________.

(A) school

(B) the park

(C) the library

(D) the swimming pool

해석 나는 **수영장**에 가는 것을 좋아해.

(A) 학교

(B) 공원

(C) 도서관

(D) 수영장

풀이 그림의 아이들이 수영장에 있으므로 답은 (D)이다.

7. There is a picture __________ the lamps.

(A) across

(B) into

(C) between

(D) in front of

해석 전등 **사이에** 그림이 있다.

(A) ~를 가로질러

(B) ~안으로

(C) ~사이에

(D) ~앞에

풀이 그림의 그림은 두 전등 사이에 있으므로 답은 (C)이다.

8. This is my __________________ Jane.

(A) older sister

(B) baby sister

(C) big brother

(D) older brother

해석 이 사람은 내 **여동생** Jane이야.

(A) 언니(누나)

(B) 여동생

(C) 오빠(형)

(D) 오빠(형)

풀이 그림에서 Jane라고 표시된 아이는 그림에서 표시된 Me보다 나이가 어리므로 답은 (B)이다.

9. They are ________________.

(A) watching TV

(B) eating breakfast

(C) talking to their parents

(D) doing their homework

해석 그들은 **숙제를 하고 있다.**

(A) TV를 본다

(B) 아침을 먹는다

(C) 그들의 부모와 대화를 한다

(D) 숙제를 한다

풀이 그림의 아이들은 공부를 하고 있으므로 답은 (D)이다.

10. My father __________________ than my mother.

(A) is cute

(B) is taller

(C) is fastest

(D) was short

해석 아버지는 어머니보다 **키가 더 크다.**

(A) 귀엽다

(B) 키가 더 크다

(C) 가장 빠르다

(D) 작았다

풀이 than을 사용하여 '아빠가 엄마보다 더 ~하다'라고 했으므로 가장 적절한 답은 비교급을 사용한 (B)이다.

Words and Phrases than ~보다 taller 더 큰 fastest 가장 빠른

Part C. Practical Reading and Retelling (p.74)

[11–12]

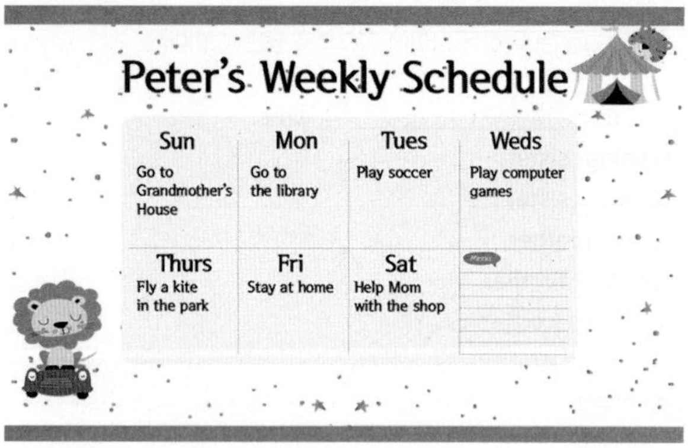

11. What does Peter do on Mondays?
(A) stay at home
(B) go to the library
(C) help Mom with the shop
(D) go to the Grandmother's house

12. What does Peter NOT have on his schedule?
(A) play soccer
(B) ride a bike
(C) fly a kite in the park
(D) play computer games

해석 Peter의 주간 일정

일요일	월요일	화요일	수요일
할머니댁에 가기	도서관 가기	축구하기	컴퓨터 게임하기
목요일	금요일	토요일	
공원에서 연 날리기	집에 있기	가게에서 엄마를 돕기	

11. Peter은 월요일에 무엇을 합니까?
(A) 집에 있는다
(B) 도서관에 간다
(C) 엄마 쇼핑을 도와드린다
(D) 할머니 댁에 간다

12. Peter의 스케줄에 없는 것은 무엇입니까?
(A) 축구하다
(B) 자전거타다
(C) 공원에서 연 날리다
(D) 컴퓨터 게임하다

풀이 스케줄에 따르면 Peter은 월요일에 도서관에 가므로 11번의 답은 (B)이다. Peter의 스케줄에 자전거타기는 없으므로 12번의 답은 (B)이다.

[13–14]

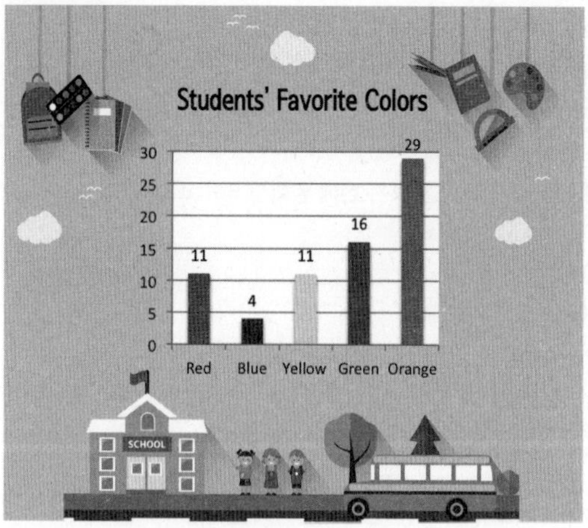

13. How many students like red?
(A) 4
(B) 11
(C) 17
(D) 29

14. What color do the students like the least?
(A) red
(B) orange
(C) green
(D) blue

해석 학생들이 가장 좋아하는 색

빨강	파랑	노랑	초록	주황
11	4	11	16	29

13. 몇 명의 학생이 빨간색을 좋아합니까?
(A) 4
(B) 11
(C) 17
(D) 29

14. 학생들이 가장 덜 좋아하는 색은 어떤 색입니까?
(A) 빨간색
(B) 주황색
(C) 초록색
(D) 파란색

풀이 빨간색을 좋아하는 학생은 11명이므로 13번의 답은 (B)이다. 파란색은 총 4명이 좋아하므로 가장 적은 학생들이 좋아한다. 따라서 14번의 답은 (D)이다.

[15–16]

15. What are they doing?
(A) playing soccer
(B) studying English
(C) making speeches
(D) playing musical instruments

16. Who is wearing a blue T-shirt?
(A) Sam
(B) Peter
(C) Annie
(D) Sophie

해석 15. 그들은 무엇을 하고 있습니까?
(A) 축구하다
(B) 영어 공부하다
(C) 연설하다
(D) 악기 연주하다

16. 파란색 티셔츠를 입고 있는 것은 누구입니까?
(A) Sam
(B) Peter
(C) Annie
(D) Sophie

풀이 그림의 사람들은 악기를 연주하고 있으므로 15번의 답은 (D)이다. Sam이 파란색 티셔츠를 입고 있으므로 16번의 답은 (A)이다.

[17–18]

17. Where do British people get on the bus?
(A) at the front door
(B) at the middle door
(C) at the back door
(D) at any door

18. What do British people do to get off the bus?
(A) stand up
(B) press the bell
(C) say 'Excuse me?'
(D) talk to the driver

해석 영국에서 버스 이용하기
1. 항상 앞문으로 버스를 타세요.
2. 버스에 탈 때 운전기사에게 돈을 내세요.
3. 앉으세요.
4. 버스가 멈추기를 원하면 벨을 누르세요.
5. 버스 중앙의 문을 사용하여 버스에서 내리세요.

17. 영국 사람들은 버스를 어디로 탑니까?
(A) 앞문
(B) 중간문
(C) 뒷문
(D) 아무 문이나

18. 버스에서 내리기 위해 영국 사람들은 무엇을 합니까?
(A) 일어나다
(B) 벨을 누르다
(C) '실례합니다'라고 말하다
(D) 운전기사에게 말하다

풀이 앞문으로 탄다고 했으므로 17번의 답은 (A)이다. 버스가 멈추기를 원하면 벨을 누르라고 했으므로 18번의 답은 (B)이다.

Words and Phrases take a seat 자리에 앉다 front 앞면
middle 중앙, 한가운데

[19–20]

19. What day is the school fair?

(A) Friday
(B) Saturday
(C) Sunday
(D) Monday

20. What can you NOT do at the fair?

(A) play games
(B) win fish
(C) play basketball
(D) eat some homemade food

해석 학교 축제
당신은 게임을 하고, 금붕어를 (상품으로) 타고, 집에서 만든 음식을 먹을 수 있습니다!
이번 주 학교 축제에 오세요!
다른 학생들, 학부모들, 선생님들을 이 즐거운 날 만나세요!
날짜: 5월 10일 토요일
시간: 오후 1시 – 4시
비용: 4달러

19. 학교 축제는 무슨 요일입니까?
(A) 금요일
(B) 토요일
(C) 일요일
(D) 월요일

20. 축제에서 무엇을 할 수 없습니까?
(A) 게임하기
(B) 물고기를 (상품으로) 타기
(C) 농구하기
(D) 집에서 만든 음식을 먹기

풀이 5월 10일 토요일이라고 했으므로 19번의 답은 (B)이다. 축제에서는 농구를 할 수 있다는 말이 없으므로 20번의 답은 (C)이다.

Words and Phrases fair 축제 goldfish 금붕어
homemade 집에서 만든, 손으로 만든

Part D. General Reading and Retelling (p.79)

[21–22]

It is my birthday today. I am ten years old. There will be a party at my house today at 1 o'clock. My friends are coming to my house to play! My mom is making pizza and lemonade. We will also eat cake and ice cream! After eating, we will sing and dance all day.

21. What will Mom make for the party?

(A) pizza
(B) cake
(C) ice cream
(D) sandwiches

22. Where is the party?

(A) the park
(B) a restaurant
(C) his school
(D) his house

해석 오늘은 내 생일이다. 나는 10살이다. 오늘 1시에 우리집에서 파티가 있을 것이다. 내 친구들은 우리 집에 놀러 온다. 엄마는 피자와 레모네이드를 만든다! 우리는 케이크와 아이스크림도 먹을 것이다! 먹고 난 다음 우리는 하루 종일 노래하고 춤을 출 것이다.

21. 엄마는 파티를 위해 무엇을 만들 것입니까?
(A) 피자
(B) 케이크
(C) 아이스크림
(D) 샌드위치

22. 파티는 어디에서 할 것입니까?
(A) 공원
(B) 레스토랑
(C) 그의 학교
(D) 그의 집

풀이 엄마는 피자와 레모네이드를 만든다고 했으므로 21번의 답은 (A)이다. 집에서 파티를 한다고 했으므로 22번의 답은 (D)이다.

[23–24]

London is the biggest city in England. There is a famous clock called Big Ben. You can see it in many pictures and movies. London also has the River Thames that goes through the city. People can take boat trips on the river and take photos of famous buildings.

23. What is Big Ben?

(A) a clock
(B) a river
(C) a boat
(D) a city

24. What can you do on the River Thames?

(A) have a picnic
(B) take your coat
(C) take a boat trip
(D) make a building

해석 런던은 영국에서 가장 큰 도시이다. Big Ben이라 불리는 유명한 시계가 있다. 당신은 많은 사진과 영화에서 그것을 볼 수 있다. 런던은 또한 도시를 가로지르는 Thames 강이 있다. 사람들은 강에서 보트 여행을 하고 유명한 건물들의 사진을 찍을 수 있다.

23. Big Ben은 무엇입니까?
(A) 시계
(B) 강
(C) 보트
(D) 도시

24. Thames 강에서 무엇을 할 수 있습니까?
(A) 소풍을 가다
(B) 코트를 가져가다
(C) 보트 여행을 하다
(D) 건물을 짓다

풀이 Big Ben은 런던에 있는 유명한 시계라고 했으므로 23번의 답은 (A)이다. 보트 여행을 하면서 유명한 건물들의 사진을 찍을 수 있다고 했으므로 24번의 답은 (C)이다.

Words and Phrases go through 관통하다 trip 여행

[25–26]
Valentine's Day is celebrated in many countries. Valentine's Day is on February 14th every year. In America and Canada, boys and girls give each other Valentine's Day cards and flowers and go to dinner. In Asia, girls give boys chocolates and other gifts. The boys then give girls gifts on White Day, which is on March 14th.

25. When is Valentine's Day?
(A) after White Day
(B) March
(C) February
(D) every month

26. What happens on White Day in Asia?
(A) There are no gifts.
(B) Girls give boys gifts.
(C) Boys give girls gifts.
(D) They give gifts to each other.

해석 발렌타인데이는 많은 나라에서 기념된다. 발렌타인데이는 매년 2월 14일에 있다. 미국과 캐나다에서는 소년과 소녀들이 발렌타인데이에 서로 카드와 꽃을 주고 저녁을 먹으러 간다. 아시아에서는, 소녀들이 소년들에게 초콜릿과 다른 선물을 준다. 소년들은 이후 3월 14일에 있는 화이트데이에 소녀들에게 선물을 준다.

25. 발렌타인데이는 언제입니까?
(A) 화이트데이 이후
(B) 3월
(C) 2월
(D) 매달

26. 아시아에서 화이트데이에 어떤 일이 일어납니까?
(A) 선물이 없다.
(B) 소녀가 소년에게 선물을 준다.
(C) 소년이 소녀에게 선물을 준다.
(D) 그들은 서로에게 선물을 준다.

풀이 발렌타인데이는 2월 14일이라고 했으므로 25번의 답은 (C)이다. 화이트데이에는 소년이 소녀에게 선물을 주므로 26번의 답은 (C)이다.

Words and Phrases celebrate 축하하다, 기념하다 each other 서로

[27–28]
Sam has a sister. Her name is Donna. Sam and Donna play together every day. Donna likes to sing and play soccer. Sam likes to play baseball and go swimming. Sam and Donna always go to the park together. They play for many hours and always go back home late.

27. Who likes soccer?
(A) Sam
(B) Donna
(C) both of them
(D) neither of them

28. How often do they play?
(A) always
(B) never
(C) rarely
(D) sometimes

해석 Sam은 여동생이 있다. 그녀의 이름은 Donna이다. Sam과 Donna는 매일 함께 논다. Donna는 노래하고 축구를 하는 것을 좋아한다. Sam은 야구하고 수영하는 것을 좋아한다. Sam과 Donna는 항상 공원에 같이 간다. 그들은 많은 시간 동안 놀고 집에 늦게 간다.

27. 누가 축구를 좋아합니까?
(A) Sam
(B) Donna
(C) 둘 다
(D) 둘 중 아무도 좋아하지 않음

28. 그들은 얼마나 자주 놉니까?
(A) 항상
(B) 절대 놀지 않는다
(C) 드물게
(D) 가끔

풀이 Donna가 축구를 좋아한다고 했으므로 27번의 답은 (B)이다. Sam과 Donna는 매일 논다고 했으므로 28번의 답은 (A)이다.

Words and Phrases always 항상

[29–30]
James has a busy day today. He has to go to school and study English, history, and math. Afterwards, James will take the bus

to town and go to the library. He has to return his library books. He will then go to the store, and his mother will buy him a hat.

29. Where does James NOT have to go today?

(A) school

(B) the store

(C) the library

(D) the train station

30. What will his mother buy him?

(A) a bag

(B) a hat

(C) a bus

(D) a book

해석 James는 오늘 바쁘다. 그는 학교에 가서 영어, 역사 그리고 수학을 공부해야 한다. 후에, James는 버스를 타고 시내에 가서 도서관에 갈 것이다. 그는 도서관 책을 반납해야 한다. 그리고 그는 가게에 갈 것이고, 엄마가 모자를 사 줄 것이다.

29. James는 오늘 어디에 가지 않아도 됩니까?

(A) 학교

(B) 가게

(C) 도서관

(D) 기차역

30. 엄마는 그에게 무엇을 사줄 것입니까?

(A) 가방

(B) 모자

(C) 버스

(D) 책

풀이 James는 오늘 버스를 타고 시내에 가므로 기차역에 갈 일은 없다. 따라서 29번의 답은 (D)이다. 엄마는 모자를 사준다고 했으므로 30번의 답은 (B)이다.

Words and Phrases afterwards 나중에, 그 뒤에 return 반납하다

TOSEL BASIC

실전 4회

Section I Listening and Speaking

1 **(D)**	2 **(A)**	3 **(B)**	4 **(D)**	5 **(C)**
6 **(B)**	7 **(C)**	8 **(A)**	9 **(C)**	10 **(B)**
11 **(A)**	12 **(C)**	13 **(D)**	14 **(D)**	15 **(B)**
16 **(A)**	17 **(D)**	18 **(A)**	19 **(C)**	20 **(A)**
21 **(B)**	22 **(B)**	23 **(A)**	24 **(B)**	25 **(A)**
26 **(C)**	27 **(D)**	28 **(A)**	29 **(B)**	30 **(C)**

Section II Reading and Writing

1 **(C)**	2 **(B)**	3 **(A)**	4 **(B)**	5 **(B)**
6 **(C)**	7 **(D)**	8 **(B)**	9 **(B)**	10 **(A)**
11 **(C)**	12 **(D)**	13 **(A)**	14 **(D)**	15 **(B)**
16 **(D)**	17 **(A)**	18 **(D)**	19 **(B)**	20 **(A)**
21 **(B)**	22 **(D)**	23 **(A)**	24 **(C)**	25 **(A)**
26 **(D)**	27 **(C)**	28 **(B)**	29 **(B)**	30 **(A)**

SECTION I LISTENING AND SPEAKING

Part A. Listen and Recognize (p.86)

1. Girl: The man is playing golf.
   (D)

해석 소녀: 남자가 골프를 치고 있다.
풀이 골프를 치는 남자 그림 (D)가 정답이다.

2. Boy: The chicken is in a pan.
   (A)

해석 소년: 닭이 후라이팬 안에 있다.
풀이 후라이팬 안에 닭이 있는 그림 (A)가 정답이다.

3. Girl: The woman is cleaning up leaves.
   (B)

해석 소녀: 여자가 나뭇잎을 치우고 있다.
풀이 갈퀴로 나뭇잎을 치우는 그림 (B)가 정답이다.

4. Boy: There are three people in the car.
   (D)

해석 소년: 차에 3명이 있다.
풀이 차 안에 3명이 있는 그림 (D)가 정답이다.

5. Girl: The sun is behind the clouds.
   (C)

해석 소녀: 해가 구름 뒤에 있다.
풀이 해가 구름 뒤에 있는 그림 (C)가 정답이다.

PART B. Listen and Respond (p.88)

6. Boy: Is sausage your favorite food?
   Girl: ______________
   (A) Yes, I am.
   (B) Yes, it is.
   (C) No, it doesn't.
   (D) No, I can't.

해석 소년: 네가 가장 좋아하는 음식이 소시지야?
소녀: ______________
(A) 응, 난 맞아.
(B) 응, 그것 맞아.
(C) 아니, 그거 안 그래.
(D) 아니, 난 할 수 없어.
풀이 소시지는 3인칭 단수이고, 사물이므로 대명사 it을 사용하고 be동사를 사용하여 질문하였으므로 대답에도 be동사가 들어간 (B)가 정답이다.

7. Girl: Where is your textbook?
   Boy: ______________
   (A) It's very thick.
   (B) It's blue and red.
   (C) It's in my backpack.
   (D) It's my favorite book.

해석 소녀: 네 교과서 어디에 있어?
소년: ______________
(A) 그것은 매우 두꺼워.
(B) 그것은 파랗고 빨개.
(C) 그것은 내 가방 안에 있어.
(D) 그것은 내가 가장 좋아하는 책이야.
풀이 교과서의 위치를 물었으므로 답은 (C)이다.

8. Boy: When did you start skating today?
   Girl: ______________
   (A) At two o'clock.
   (B) On the lake.
   (C) For one week.
   (D) Tomorrow morning.

해석 소년: 오늘 스케이트 언제 타기 시작했어?
소녀: ______________
(A) 2시에.
(B) 호수에서.
(C) 1주일 동안.
(D) 내일 아침.
풀이 스케이트를 타기 시작한 시간을 묻는 것이므로 답은 (A)이다.

9. Girl: How much are those chocolates?
   Boy: ______________
   (A) There are twelve in it.
   (B) There are 10 boxes.

(C) It's twenty-nine dollars.
(D) It's 30 centimeters long.

해석 소녀: 저 초콜릿 얼마예요?
소년: ________________
(A) 12개 들었어요.
(B) 10박스 있어요.
(C) 29달러예요.
(D) 30cm이에요.

풀이 초콜릿의 가격을 물었으므로 답은 (C)이다.

10. Boy: Why do you look so happy?
Girl: ________________
(A) My dog died yesterday.
(B) I got a new computer.
(C) I couldn't sleep.
(D) My homework is hard.

해석 소년: 왜 그렇게 행복해 보여?
소녀: ________________
(A) 내 개가 어제 죽었어.
(B) 나는 새 컴퓨터를 샀어.
(C) 나는 잠을 잘 수가 없었어.
(D) 내 숙제가 어려워.

풀이 행복해 보이는 이유로 보기 중 가장 적절한 것은 (B)이다.

Part C. Listen and Retell (p.89)

11. Girl: I don't see Brenda.
Boy: She's in the restroom.
Question: Where is Brenda?
(A)

해석 소녀: Brenda가 안 보이네.
소년: 그녀는 화장실에 있어.
질문: Brenda는 어디에 있습니까?

풀이 Brenda는 화장실에 있다고 했으므로 답은 (A)이다.

Words and Phrases restroom 화장실

12. Boy: What do you want to drink?
Girl: Some water, please.
Question: What does the girl want?
(C)

해석 소년: 뭐 마실래?
소녀: 물 좀 줘.
질문: 소녀는 무엇을 원합니까?

풀이 소녀는 물을 원한다고 했으므로 답은 (C)이다.

13. Girl: Is your father a doctor?
Boy: Yes, he is.
Question: Who is the boy's father?
(D)

해석 소녀: 네 아버지는 의사이시니?
소년: 응, 그는 의사야.
질문: 소년의 아버지는 누구입니까?

풀이 소년의 아버지는 의사라고 했으므로 답은 (D)이다.

14. Boy: Where's my favorite cup?
Girl: It's in the sink.
Question: Where is the boy's cup?
(A) It's on the floor.
(B) It's on the table.
(C) It's in the cupboard.
(D) It's in the sink.

해석 소년: 내가 가장 좋아하는 컵이 어디에 있니?
소녀: 싱크대 안에 있어.
질문: 소년의 컵은 어디 있습니까?
(A) 그것은 바닥에 있다.
(B) 그것은 테이블 위에 있다.
(C) 그것은 찬장 안에 있다.
(D) 그것은 싱크대 안에 있다.

풀이 컵이 싱크대 안에 있다고 했으므로 답은 (D)다.

Words and Phrases sink 싱크대

15. Girl: My stomach hurts.
Boy: Why don't you take a break?
Question: What's wrong with the girl?
(A) She has a headache.
(B) She has a stomachache.
(C) Her leg hurts.
(D) Her neck hurts.

해석 소녀: 배가 아파.
소년: 잠시 쉬는 것은 어때?
질문: 소녀에게 어떤 문제가 있습니까?
(A) 그녀는 두통이 있다.
(B) 그녀는 복통이 있다.
(C) 그녀의 다리가 아프다.
(D) 그녀의 목이 아프다.

풀이 소녀는 배가 아프다고 했으므로 답은 (B)이다.

Words and Phrases stomachache 복통 headache 두통
take a rest 쉬다, 휴식을 취하다

16. Boy: Let's go down the slide.
Girl: No, I want to go on the swings.
Question: Where are they?
(A) at a playground
(B) at a store
(C) in a classroom
(D) in a car

해석 소년: 미끄럼틀 타자.
소녀: 아니야, 나는 그네를 타고 싶어.
질문: 그들은 어디에 있습니까?
(A) 놀이터에
(B) 가게에
(C) 교실에
(D) 차안에

풀이 미끄럼틀과 그네가 있는 곳은 놀이터이므로 답은 (A)이다.

Words and Phrases swing 그네

17. Girl: I like the red sweater.
Boy: I like the blue shirt.
Question: What does the boy like?
(A) the red sweater
(B) the blue sweater
(C) the red shirt
(D) the blue shirt

해석 소녀: 나는 빨간 스웨터가 좋아.
소년: 나는 파란 셔츠가 좋아.
질문: 소년은 무엇을 좋아합니까?
(A) 빨간 스웨터
(B) 파란 스웨터
(C) 빨간 셔츠
(D) 파란 셔츠

풀이 소년은 파란 셔츠가 좋다고 했으므로 답은 (D)이다.

[18–19]
Boy: At school, I eat a snack at 10:00 every morning. My favorite snack is a bag of potato chips, but now I cannot eat them at school. They are not healthy and students can only bring healthy snacks. Fruit, cheese, and vegetables are okay, though.

18. When does the boy eat a snack at school?
(A) at 10:00 AM
(B) at 10:30 AM
(C) at 11:00 AM
(D) at 11:30 AM

19. What can the boy NOT eat at school?
(A) vegetables
(B) cheese
(C) potato chips
(D) fruit

해석 소년: 학교에서 나는 매일 아침 10시에 간식을 먹는다. 내가 가장 좋아하는 간식은 감자칩 한 봉지인데, 나는 학교에서 그것을 먹을 수 없다. 그것은 건강에 좋지 않고 학생들은 건강한 간식만 가져올 수 있다. 그러나 과일, 치즈, 야채는 괜찮다.

18. 소년은 학교에서 언제 간식을 먹습니까?
(A) 오전 10시에
(B) 오전 10시 30분에
(C) 오전 11시에
(D) 오전 11시 30분에

19. 소년은 학교에서 무엇을 먹을 수 없습니까?
(A) 야채
(B) 치즈
(C) 감자칩
(D) 과일

풀이 소년은 아침 10시에 간식을 먹는다고 했으므로 18번의 답은 (A)이다. 감자칩은 건강하지 않아서 안된다고 했으므로 19번의 답은 (C)이다.

Words and Phrases though 그러나

[20–21]
Girl: Last night there was a dance party at my school. Each student paid $3.00 to enter. The money will be used by the school. They will build a new school playground. The party was fun. There were many games and lots of food. I danced with my friends, too.

20. How much did each student pay?
(A) $3.00
(B) $6.00
(C) $9.00
(D) $10.00

21. What will the school do with the ticket money?
(A) build more classrooms
(B) build a new playground
(C) have more parties
(D) buy more computers

해석 소녀: 지난 밤 학교에서 춤 파티가 있었다. 각 학생은 들어가기 위해 3달러를 지불했다. 돈은 학교에 의해 쓰일 것이다. 그들은 새로운 학교 놀이터를 지을 것이다. 파티는 재미있었다. 많은 게임과 음식이 있었다. 나는 또한 내 친구들과 춤을 추었다.

20. 각 학생은 얼마를 지불했습니까?
(A) 3달러
(B) 6달러
(C) 9달러
(D) 10달러

21. 학교는 티켓 돈으로 무엇을 할 것입니까?
(A) 교실을 더 짓는다
(B) 새 놀이터를 짓는다
(C) 더 많은 파티를 연다
(D) 컴퓨터를 더 산다

풀이 입장료는 3달러이므로 20번의 답은 (A)이다. 학교는 새로운 놀이터를 짓는다고 했으므로 21번의 답은 (B)이다.

Words and Phrases lots of 많은

[22–23]
Boy: I love watching movies. Someday, I want to be an actor. These days, I go to an acting school on Sunday mornings. We learn how to speak and act. We are preparing for a play called Alice in Wonderland. My parents are excited to see our play next month.

22. What does the boy want to be?
(A) an author
(B) an actor
(C) a musician

(D) a teacher

23. Why are the boy's parents excited?

(A) The boy will be in a play.
(B) The boy will get good grades.
(C) They will see a movie.
(D) They will go to an acting school.

해석 소년: 나는 영화를 보는 것을 좋아한다. 언젠가, 나는 배우가 되고 싶다. 요즘, 나는 일요일 아침마다 연기 학원에 간다. 우리는 어떻게 말하고 연기하는지 배운다. 우리는 이상한 나라의 앨리스라는 연극을 준비한다. 부모님은 다음 달에 우리의 연극을 보게 되어 기뻐 하신다.

22. 소년은 무엇이 되고 싶어합니까?
(A) 작가
(B) 배우
(C) 음악가
(D) 교사

23. 왜 소년의 부모님이 기쁩니까?
(A) 소년이 연극에 출연할 것이다.
(B) 소년은 좋은 점수를 받을 것이다.
(C) 그들은 영화를 볼 것이다.
(D) 그들은 연기 학원에 갈 것이다.

풀이 소년은 배우가 되고 싶다고 했으므로 22번의 답은 (B)이다. 다음 달에 소년의 연극을 보게 되어 기쁘다고 했으므로 23번의 답은 (A)이다.

Words and Phrases play 연극 grade 성적 learn 배우다 prepare 준비하다

[24–25]

Girl: I live in northern Canada. My small hometown is called Yellowknife. In December, we only have 5 hours of sunshine every day. It gets very cold in the winter. The icy wind can freeze your skin, so I wear a warm coat made of fur. I also wear a scarf, mittens, and a hat.

24. How many hours of sunshine does Yellowknife have in December?

(A) four hours every day
(B) five hours every day
(C) nine hours every day
(D) fifteen hours every day

25. What clothing does the girl NOT talk about?

(A) boots
(B) hat
(C) scarf
(D) mittens

해석 소녀: 나는 캐나다 북부에 산다. 나의 작은 고향은 Yellowknife라 불린다. 12월에는, 매일 5시간만 햇살이 난다. 겨울에는 매우 추워진다. 얼음 같은 바람은 피부를 얼릴 수 있어서 나는 털로 만든 따뜻한 코트를 입는다. 나는 또한 스카프, 장갑, 모자를 착용한다.

24. 12월에 Yellowknife에는 몇 시간의 햇살이 있습니까?
(A) 매일 4시간
(B) 매일 5시간
(C) 매일 9시간
(D) 매일 15시간

25. 소녀는 어떤 의복에 대해 말하지 않았습니까?
(A) 부츠
(B) 모자
(C) 스카프
(D) 장갑

풀이 12월에는 5시간만 햇살이 나온다고 했으므로 24번의 답은 (B)이다. 소녀는 스카프, 장갑, 모자에 대해 말했으므로 25번의 답은 (A)이다.

Part D. Listen and Speak (p.93)

26. Boy: Look at my pants!
Girl: What is that black spot?
Boy: It's oil from the street.
Girl: ____________________

(A) I need a bath.
(B) That looks great.
(C) Oh no, that's too bad.
(D) I have black socks.

해석 소년: 내 바지를 좀 봐!
소녀: 저 검은 얼룩은 뭐야?
소년: 길거리에서 묻은 기름이야.
소녀: ____________________
(A) 나는 목욕이 필요해.
(B) 좋아 보인다.
(C) 이런, 안됐다.
(D) 나는 검정색 양말이 있어.

풀이 소년의 바지의 기름 때에 대한 적절한 반응은 (C)이다.

Words and Phrases spot 얼룩

27. Girl: Jim, wait for me!
Boy: Hi, Jenny.
Girl: Why are you carrying flowers?
Boy: ____________________

(A) They're in my garden.
(B) I have a lot of homework.
(C) You missed the bus.
(D) They're for my mother.

해석 소녀: Jim, 기다려!
소년: 안녕, Jenny야.
소녀: 왜 꽃을 들고 가는거야?
소년: ____________________
(A) 그들은 내 정원에 있어.
(B) 나는 숙제가 많아.
(C) 너는 버스를 놓쳤어.
(D) 이것들은 내 어머니를 위한 거야.

풀이 꽃을 들고 가는 이유로 보기 중 가장 자연스러운 대답은 어머니를 위한 것이라고 하는 (D)이다.

Words and Phrases miss 놓치다

28. Girl: I can't find my gloves!
Boy: Oh no!
Girl: Can you help me find them?
Boy: ________________

(A) Yes, of course.
(B) Sure, see you later.
(C) Yes, you can lose them.
(D) I didn't know that.

해석 소녀: 장갑을 못 찾겠어!
소년: 이런!
소녀: 내가 찾는 것을 도와줄 수 있니?
소년: ____________
(A) 응, 당연하지.
(B) 응, 나중에 보자.
(C) 응, 너는 잃어버릴 수 있어.
(D) 나는 몰랐어.

풀이 찾는 것을 도와줄 수 있는지 묻는 말에 적절한 대답은 (A)이다.

29. Boy: Did you read this book?
Girl: Yes, I did.
Boy: How was it?
Girl: ________________

(A) They're interesting.
(B) It's a little boring.
(C) It's the best song.
(D) They sell books.

해석 소년: 이 책을 읽었니?
소녀: 응, 읽었어.
소년: 어땠어?
소녀: ____________
(A) 그것들은 흥미로워.
(B) 조금 지루해.
(C) 가장 좋은 노래야.
(D) 그들은 책을 팔아.

풀이 책이 어떤지는 3인칭 단수 대명사인 it을 사용하여 물어보았으므로 it을 사용하여 대답한 (B)가 답이다. (C)는 it을 사용하여 대답하였으나 book이 아닌 song이라고 하였으므로 오답이다.

30. Boy: Can you help me with my science project?
Girl: Sorry, I'm too busy all week.
Boy: Do you have time on Friday?
Girl: ________________

(A) No, I don't know you.
(B) I'm free every day.
(C) No, I don't. Sorry.
(D) It's three-thirty.

해석 소년: 내 과학 프로젝트를 도와줄 수 있니?
소녀: 미안해, 나는 이번주 내내 바빠.
소년: 금요일에 시간 있어?
소녀: ____________
(A) 아니, 난 널 몰라.
(B) 나는 매일 시간이 많아.
(C) 아니, 없어. 미안해.
(D) 3시 30분이야.

풀이 소녀는 이번주 내내 바쁘다고 했으므로 적절한 답은 (C)이다.

SECTION II READING AND WRITING

Part A. Sentence Completion (p.96)

1. A: What is Dad doing in the kitchen?
B: He's ________ the dishes.

(A) do
(B) does
(C) doing
(D) doed

해석 A: 아빠가 부엌에서 뭐 하셔?
B: 설거지 **하고 계셔.**
(A) 하다
(B) 하다(3인칭 단수)
(C) 하고 있는
(D) 틀린 표현

풀이 A가 아빠가 부엌에서 무엇을 하고 있는지 현재진행형으로 물어봤으므로 현재진행형이 와야 한다. 따라서 답은 (C)이다.

2. A: ________ is the name of your dog?
B: It's Matilda.

(A) Who
(B) What
(C) When
(D) Where

해석 A: 너의 개의 이름이 **무엇**이니?
B: Matilda야.
(A) 누구
(B) 무엇
(C) 언제
(D) 어디

풀이 B의 답을 보아 이름이 무엇인지 묻는 것이 가장 자연스러우므로 답은 (B)이다.

3. A: Come join the baseball team.
B: Sorry, I'm not very good __________ sports.

(A) at
(B) by
(C) to
(D) of

해석 A: 야구 팀에 가입해.
B: 미안, 나는 운동을 잘 하지 못해.
(A) ~에
(B) ~옆에
(C) ~로
(D) ~의

풀이 '~를 잘하다'는 'be good at'으로 쓰므로 답은 (A)이다.

4. A: Can we walk to John's house?
B: No, it's too far __________.
(A) walk
(B) to walk
(C) walking
(D) will walk

해석 A: 우리 John의 집으로 걸어갈 수 있니?
B: 아니, **걷기엔** 너무 멀어.
(A) 걷다
(B) 걷기에
(C) 걷는
(D) 걸을 것이다

풀이 'too + 형용사 + to + 동사원형'은 '~하기에는 ~하다'의 뜻으로 빈칸에는 'to + 동사원형' 형태가 와야 한다. 따라서 답은 (B)이다.

5. A: ________ you turn on the fan? I'm hot.
B: Really? Not me. I feel cold.
(A) Do
(B) Can
(C) Does
(D) Should

해석 A: 선풍기 틀어**줄 수 있어**? 더워.
B: 정말? 난 아닌데. 나는 추워.
(A) 조동사 Do
(B) 조동사 Can
(C) 조동사 Does
(D) 조동사 Should

풀이 A는 선풍기를 켜달라는 요청을 하고 싶으므로 '~(할) 수 있어?'라는 뜻의 'Can'이 와야 한다. 따라서 답은 (B)이다.

Part B. Situational Writing (p.97)

6. The woman is __________________.
(A) setting a table
(B) playing the piano
(C) painting a picture
(D) listening to music

해석 여자는 **그림을 그리고 있다.**
(A) 상을 차리다
(B) 피아노를 치다
(C) 그림을 그리다
(D) 음악을 듣다

풀이 그림의 여자는 그림을 그리고 있으므로 답은 (C)이다.

7. The children are __________________ the rollercoaster.
(A) waiting in line for
(B) getting on
(C) getting off
(D) riding

해석 아이들은 롤러코스터를 **타고 있다.**
(A) 줄을 서서 기다리고 있다
(B) 타고 있다
(C) 내리고 있다
(D) 타는 중이다

풀이 그림의 아이들은 롤러코스터를 타는 중이므로 답은 (D)이다.

8. The family is __________________.
(A) throwing snowballs
(B) building a snowman
(C) sliding down a snowy hill
(D) clearing snow off the road

해석 가족은 **눈사람을 만들고 있다.**
(A) 눈뭉치를 던진다
(B) 눈사람을 만든다
(C) 눈내린 언덕을 미끄러져 내려온다
(D) 길의 눈을 치운다

풀이 그림의 가족은 눈사람을 만들고 있으므로 답은 (B)이다.

Words and Phrases clear off 치우다 throw 던지다

9. The girl is wearing ____________.
(A) white mittens
(B) blue pants
(C) a green hat
(D) a pink coat

해석 여자는 **파란 바지**를 입고있다.
(A) 하얀 장갑
(B) 파란 바지
(C) 초록 모자
(D) 분홍 코트

풀이 여자는 파란 바지를 입고 있으므로 답은 (B)이다.

10. The woman is __________________.
(A) reading a magazine
(B) reading a newspaper
(C) talking on a phone
(D) talking to a nurse

해석 여자는 **잡지를 읽고 있다.**
(A) 잡지를 읽고 있다
(B) 신문을 읽고 있다
(C) 전화하고 있다
(D) 간호사와 얘기하고 있다

풀이 그림의 여자는 잡지를 읽고 있으므로 답은 (A)이다.

Part C. Practical Reading and Retelling (p.99)

[11–12]

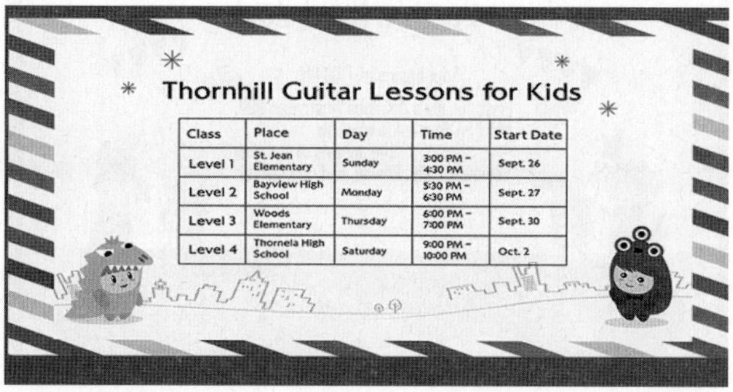
Thornhill Guitar Lessons for Kids

Class	Place	Day	Time	Start Date
Level 1	St. Jean Elementary	Sunday	3:00 PM - 4:30 PM	Sept. 26
Level 2	Bayview High School	Monday	5:30 PM - 6:30 PM	Sept. 27
Level 3	Woods Elementary	Thursday	6:00 PM - 7:00 PM	Sept. 30
Level 4	Thornela High School	Saturday	9:00 PM - 10:00 PM	Oct. 2

11. What starts on Sept. 30?
 (A) Level 1
 (B) Level 2
 (C) Level 3
 (D) Level 4

12. Where are Saturday lessons offered?
 (A) at St. Jean Elementary
 (B) at Bayview High School
 (C) at Woods Elementary
 (D) at Thornela High School

해석 11. 9월 30일에 무엇이 시작합니까?
 (A) 레벨 1
 (B) 레벨 2
 (C) 레벨 3
 (D) 레벨 4

 12. 토요일 수업은 어디에서 제공됩니까?
 (A) St. Jean 초등학교
 (B) Bayview 고등학교
 (C) Woods 초등학교
 (D) Thornela 고등학교

풀이 레벨 3이 9월 30일에 시작하므로 11번의 답은 (C)이다. 토요일 수업은 Thornela 고등학교에서 하므로 12번의 답은 (D)이다.

Words and Phrases offer 제공하다

[13–14]

Bowling Club Rates

Day	TIME	PRICE for 1 GAME
Monday - Friday	9:00 AM - 6:00 PM	$3.00
Monday - Thursday	6:00 PM - 11:00 PM	$4.50
Friday - Saturday	6:00 PM - 11:00 PM	$5.50
Sunday Special	9:00 AM - 9:00 PM	$3.50

13. When is it cheapest to bowl?
 (A) Monday - Friday daytime
 (B) Monday - Thursday evening
 (C) Friday - Saturday evening
 (D) all day Sunday

14. How much does one game cost on a Friday night?
 (A) $3.00
 (B) $3.50
 (C) $4.50
 (D) $5.50

해석

요일	시간	1게임당 가격
월요일 – 금요일	오전 9:00 – 오후 6:00	3달러
월요일 – 목요일	오후 6:00 – 오후 11:00	4.5달러
금요일 – 토요일	오후 6:00 – 오후 11:00	5.5달러
일요일 특별가	오전 9:00 – 오후 9:00	3.5달러

 13. 볼링을 치기에 가장 저렴할 때는 언제입니까?
 (A) 월요일 – 금요일 낮
 (B) 월요일 – 목요일 저녁
 (C) 금요일 – 토요일 저녁
 (D) 일요일 하루 종일

 14. 금요일 밤에는 한 게임이 얼마입니까?
 (A) 3달러
 (B) 3.5달러
 (C) 4.5달러
 (D) 5.5달러

풀이 가장 싼 3달러는 월요일에서 금요일까지 낮이므로 13번의 답은 (A)이다. 금요일 밤에는 한 게임당 5.5달러이므로 14번의 답은 (D)이다.

Words and Phrases rate 요금 bowl 볼링을 치다

[15-16]

15. What subject do tutors NOT teach?
(A) English
(B) history
(C) math
(D) science

16. How much is a two-hour lesson?
(A) $25.00
(B) $35.00
(C) $60.00
(D) $70.00

해석 우리는 1-12학년에게 수학, 영어, 과학을 가르칩니다.
가격 : 시간 당 35달러
위치 : 1275 Leslie 거리
우리는 방문 수업은 제공하지 않습니다.
만남을 위해서는 전화 혹은 이메일을 주세요.

15. 개인 교사가 가르치지 않는 것은 무엇입니까?
(A) 영어
(B) 역사
(C) 수학
(D) 과학

16. 2시간 레슨은 얼마입니까?
(A) 25달러
(B) 35달러
(C) 60달러
(D) 70달러

풀이 개인 교사는 수학, 영어, 과학을 가르치므로 15번의 답은 (B)이다. 1시간에 35달러이므로 두시간은 70달러이다. 따라서 16번의 답은 (D)이다.

Words and Phrases in-home 집에서 하는 set up 조율하다, 예약하다

[17-18]

17. What do visitors do first?
(A) eat dinner
(B) look at the stars
(C) look at animals at night
(D) look at animals in the day

18. What kind of animals do visitors see?
(A) snakes
(B) camels
(C) black bears
(D) koalas

해석 Perth의 야간 동물원에 오신 것을 환영합니다!
투어는 오후 7:00에 시작합니다.
먼저 : 맛있는 호주산 BBQ를 즐기세요.
다음 : 투어 가이드가 야행성 동물들을 보여줄 것입니다. 올빼미, 박쥐, 코알라, 악어를 구경하세요!

17. 방문객들은 먼저 무엇을 합니까?
(A) 저녁을 먹는다
(B) 별을 본다
(C) 밤에 동물을 본다
(D) 낮에 동물을 본다

18. 방문객은 어떤 종류의 동물을 봅니까?
(A) 뱀
(B) 낙타
(C) 흑곰
(D) 코알라

풀이 먼저 호주산 BBQ를 즐기라고 했으므로 17번의 답은 (A)이다. 올빼미, 박쥐, 코알라, 악어를 보라고 했으므로 18번의 답은 (D)이다.

Words and Phrases delicious 맛있는 camel 낙타 koala 코알라

[19–20]

19. What will students NOT learn at the camp?

(A) how to act
(B) how to draw
(C) how to take pictures
(D) how to make movies

20. How much is one week at the half-day camp?

(A) $150.00
(B) $200.00
(C) $300.00
(D) $400.00

해석 아이들을 위한 영상 제작 겨울 캠프

날짜 : 첫 번째 주. 12월 20일 – 12월 24일
두 번째 주. 12월 27일 – 12월 31일

당신은 캠프에서 이것들을 할 수 있습니다:
– 영화 만들기
– 드라마 게임하기
– 카메라 배우기
– 연기 수업듣기

비용 : 하루 종일 = 한 주에 200달러
: 반나절 = 한 주에 150달러

19. 학생들은 캠프에서 무엇을 배우지 않을 것입니까?
(A) 연기하는 방법
(B) 그림 그리는 방법
(C) 사진 찍는 방법
(D) 영화 만드는 방법

20. 반나절 캠프는 한 주에 얼마입니까?
(A) 150달러
(B) 200달러
(C) 300달러
(D) 400달러

풀이 그림 그리는 방법을 배운다는 말을 하지 않았으므로 19번의 답은 (B)이다. 반나절 캠프는 한 주에 150달러라고 했으므로 20번의 답은 (A)이다.

Words and Phrases film–making 영상제작 fee 요금

Part D. General Reading and Retelling (p.104)

[21–22]

Last night I had an interesting dream. I was playing with a balloon in my yard. Suddenly, I started to fly up into the air like a bird. I went up to the clouds. I looked down and saw the mountains. I saw the park and the river. I was not afraid. Then I woke up.

21. What did the writer see in her dream?

(A) a lake
(B) a park
(C) a library
(D) a playground

22. How did the writer feel in her dream?

(A) sad
(B) afraid
(C) worried
(D) interested

해석 지난 밤 나는 흥미로운 꿈을 꾸었다. 나는 마당에서 풍선을 가지고 놀고 있었다. 갑자기, 나는 새처럼 공기 위로 날기 시작했다. 나는 구름위로 올라갔다. 나는 내려다 보았고 산을 보았다. 나는 공원과 강을 보았다. 나는 두렵지 않았다. 그리고 나서 나는 잠에서 깨어났다.

21. 글쓴이는 꿈에서 무엇을 보았습니까?
(A) 호수
(B) 공원
(C) 도서관
(D) 놀이터

22. 글쓴이는 꿈에서 어떤 기분을 느꼈습니까?
(A) 슬픈
(B) 두려운
(C) 걱정된
(D) 흥미로운

풀이 공원과 강을 보았다고 했으므로 21번의 답은 (B)이다. 흥미로운 꿈을 꾸었다고 했으므로 22번의 답은 (D)이다.

Words and Phrases suddenly 갑자기

[23–24]

My name is Simon, and I am from England. However, these days I live in India. We move often because of my father's job. Last year we lived in Indonesia. Two years ago, we lived in China. Next year we will move to Thailand. Every year I change schools. It is not easy, because I have to make new friends each time.

23. Where does the boy live now?

(A) in India
(B) in China
(C) in England
(D) in Thailand

24. What is difficult for the boy?

(A) changing houses

(B) doing school work

(C) making new friends

(D) learning new languages

해석 내 이름은 Simon이고 영국에서 왔다. 하지만, 나는 요즘 인도에서 산다. 우리는 아버지의 직업 때문에 종종 이사한다. 지난해 우리는 인도네시아에 살았다. 2년 전 우리는 중국에서 살았다. 내년에 우리는 태국으로 이사할 것이다. 매년 나는 학교를 바꾼다. 내가 매번 새로운 친구를 사귀어야 하기 때문에 이것은 쉽지 않다.

23. 소년은 현재 어디에 삽니까?

(A) 인도에

(B) 중국에

(C) 영국에

(D) 태국에

24. 무엇이 소년에게 어렵습니까?

(A) 집을 바꾸다

(B) 학교 공부를 하다

(C) 새 친구를 사귀다

(D) 새 언어를 배우다

풀이 소년은 요즘 인도에 산다고 했으므로 23번의 답은 (A)이다.
매번 새로운 친구를 사귀는 것은 쉽지 않다고 했으므로 24번의 답은 (C)이다.

[25–26]

Bark spiders live in Madagascar. They make the largest spider webs in the world. Their webs can be over 25 meters long. Only bark spiders build their webs over rivers. Their webs catch flying insects. Bark spiders mainly eat flies and mosquitoes.

25. Where do bark spiders build their webs?

(A) over rivers

(B) on the ground

(C) in thick forests

(D) inside buildings

26. What do bark spiders mainly eat?

(A) their webs

(B) other spiders

(C) Madagascar

(D) flies and mosquitoes

해석 나무껍질 거미는 마다가스카에 산다. 그들은 세계에서 가장 큰 거미줄을 만든다. 그들의 거미줄은 25미터보다 더 길 수도 있다. 나무껍질 거미만이 거미줄을 강 위에 만든다. 그들의 거미줄은 날아다니는 곤충을 잡을 수 있다. 나무껍질 거미는 주로 파리와 모기를 먹는다.

25. 나무껍질 거미는 어디에 거미줄을 만듭니까?

(A) 강 위에

(B) 땅에

(C) 빽빽한 숲에

(D) 건물 안에

26. 나무껍질 거미는 주로 무엇을 먹습니까?

(A) 그들의 거미줄

(B) 다른 거미들

(C) 마다가스카

(D) 파리와 모기

풀이 거미줄을 강 위에 만든다고 했으므로 25번의 답은 (A)이다. 나무껍질 거미는 주로 파리와 모기를 먹는다고 했으므로 26번의 답은 (D)이다.

Words and Phrases bark 나무 껍질 web 거미줄 mosquito 모기

[27–28]

Jordan Romero was very young, but he decided to climb seven of the tallest mountains in the world. At 9 years old, Jordan climbed Mount Kilimanjaro in Tanzania. In 2010, he became the youngest person to climb the tallest mountain in the world - Mount Everest. He was just 13 years old.

27. How old was Jordan when he climbed Mount Kilimanjaro?

(A) 5 years old

(B) 7 years old

(C) 9 years old

(D) 13 years old

28. What is special about Jordan?

(A) He was the first to climb Mount Everest.

(B) He was the youngest to climb Mount Everest.

(C) He was the youngest to climb Mount Kilimanjaro.

(D) He was the first to climb seven of the tallest mountains

해석 Jordan Romero는 매우 어렸지만 세계에서 가장 큰 산 중 7개를 등반하기로 결정했다. 9살일 때, Jordan은 탄자니아에 있는 킬리만자로산을 등반했다. 2010년에는, 세계에서 가장 높은 산 에베레스트를 등반하는 가장 어린 사람이 되었다. 그는 겨우 13살이었다.

27. Jordan이 킬리만자로산을 등반할 때 몇 살이었습니까?

(A) 5살

(B) 7살

(C) 9살

(D) 13살

28. Jordan에 대한 특별한 점이 무엇입니까?

(A) 그는 에베레스트 산을 처음으로 등반한 사람이다.

(B) 그는 에베레스트 산을 등반한 가장 어린 사람이다.

(C) 그는 킬리만자로 산을 등반한 가장 어린 사람이다.

(D) 그는 가장 높은 산 중 7개를 처음으로 등반한 사람이다.

풀이 Jordan은 9살에 킬리만자로 산을등반했으므로 27번의 답은 (C)이다. Jordan은 에베레스트 산을 등반한 가장 어린 사람이라고 했으므로 28번의 답은 (B)이다.

[29–30]

Our school has a garden. My classmates and I work in the garden every day. We water the plants and keep them healthy. There are vegetables and herbs in our garden. Our school cafeteria uses the food to make delicious lunches. We enjoy eating our fresh vegetables.

29. Where is the garden?

(A) at a teacher's home

(B) at the students' school

(C) in the country

(D) in a garden center

30. What does the school do with the vegetables?

(A) use them to make lunches for kids

(B) give them to poor people

(C) sell them to the students' parents

(D) sell them at a farmers' market

해석 우리 학교에는 정원이 있다. 반 친구들과 나는 매일 정원에서 일한다. 우리는 식물에게 물을 주고 그들이 건강하도록 돌본다. 우리 정원에는 야채와 허브가 있다. 우리 학교 식당은 맛있는 점심을 만들기 위해 그 음식들을 사용한다. 우리는 우리의 신선한 야채를 먹는 것을 즐긴다.

29. 정원은 어디에 있습니까?

(A) 선생님댁에

(B) 학생들의 학교에

(C) 시골에

(D) 정원 센터에

30. 학교는 야채를 가지고 무엇을 합니까?

(A) 아이들에게 줄 점심을 만들 때 사용한다

(B) 가난한 사람들에게 준다

(C) 학생들의 부모에게 판다

(D) 농부의 시장에서 판다

풀이 정원은 학교에 있으므로 29번의 답은 (B)이다. 야채는 카페테리아에서 사용한다고 했으므로 30번의 답은 (A)이다.

TOSEL BASIC

실전 5회

Section Ⅰ Listening and Speaking

1 **(C)**	2 **(A)**	3 **(A)**	4 **(A)**	5 **(D)**
6 **(D)**	7 **(C)**	8 **(D)**	9 **(A)**	10 **(B)**
11 **(A)**	12 **(C)**	13 **(D)**	14 **(B)**	15 **(B)**
16 **(C)**	17 **(A)**	18 **(D)**	19 **(D)**	20 **(A)**
21 **(B)**	22 **(D)**	23 **(B)**	24 **(B)**	25 **(C)**
26 **(A)**	27 **(A)**	28 **(C)**	29 **(B)**	30 **(C)**

Section Ⅱ Reading and Writing

1 **(B)**	2 **(A)**	3 **(B)**	4 **(C)**	5 **(C)**
6 **(D)**	7 **(C)**	8 **(A)**	9 **(D)**	10 **(A)**
11 **(C)**	12 **(A)**	13 **(C)**	14 **(B)**	15 **(A)**
16 **(D)**	17 **(C)**	18 **(B)**	19 **(C)**	20 **(D)**
21 **(D)**	22 **(A)**	23 **(C)**	24 **(D)**	25 **(B)**
26 **(C)**	27 **(C)**	28 **(A)**	29 **(D)**	30 **(B)**

SECTION Ⅰ LISTENING AND SPEAKING

Part A. Listen and Recognize (p.111)

1. Girl: The dog is sitting in its house.
(C)
해석 소녀: 개가 그의 집에 앉아 있다.
풀이 개집에 앉아 있는 그림 (C)가 답이다.

2. Girl: The woman works at a bank.
(A)
해석 소녀: 여자는 은행에서 일한다.
풀이 은행에서 일하는 여자 그림 (A)가 답이다.

3. Boy: The boy is dreaming of a dolphin.
(A)
해석 소년: 소년은 돌고래 꿈을 꾸고 있다.
풀이 소년이 돌고래 꿈을 꾸는 그림 (A)가 답이다.

4. Girl: There is a fork on the plate.
(A)
해석 소녀: 접시 위에 포크가 있다.
풀이 접시 위에 포크가 있는 그림 (A)가 답이다.
Words and Phrases plate 접시

5. Boy: The door is open.
(D)
해석 소년: 문이 열려있다.
풀이 문이 열려 있는 그림 (D)가 답이다.

PART B. Listen and Respond (p.113)

6. Girl : Do you like fish?
Boy: ____________________
(A) Yes, I am.
(B) Yes, I can.
(C) No, I won't.
(D) No, I don't.
해석 소녀: 물고기를 좋아하니?
소년: ______________
(A) 응, 나 맞아.
(B) 응, 나 할 수 있어
(C) 아니, 나는 안 할 거야.
(D) 아니, 난 안 좋아해.
풀이 질문에 조동사 do를 사용하여 물어보았으므로, 조동사 do를 사용하여 대답한 (D)가 답이다.

7. Boy: You're crying!
Girl: ____________________
(A) That's too bad.
(B) Please don't cry.
(C) This movie is so sad.
(D) You're really interesting.
해석 소년: 너 울고 있네!
소녀: ______________
(A) 안타깝다.
(B) 제발 울지마.
(C) 이 영화는 너무 슬퍼.
(D) 너는 정말 흥미롭다.
풀이 울고 있다는 소년의 말에 보기 중 소녀의 반응으로 가장 자연스러운 것은 영화가 슬퍼서라고 말하는 (C)이다.

8. Girl: Where is the orange juice?
Boy: ____________________
(A) I like it, too.
(B) It's very sweet.
(C) It's my favorite.
(D) It's in the fridge.
해석 소녀: 오렌지 주스 어디 있어?
소년: ______________
(A) 나도 좋아.
(B) 매우 달아.
(C) 내가 가장 좋아하는 거야.
(D) 냉장고 안에 있어.
풀이 오렌지 주스의 위치를 물었으므로 적절한 답은 (D)이다.

9. Boy: Can I use your phone?

Girl: ____________________

(A) **Sure, go ahead.**

(B) Sure, I can.

(C) Sorry, it's not.

(D) No, you won't.

해석 소녀: 나 네 휴대폰 쓸 수 있어?

소녀: ________________

(A) 물론, 어서 사용해.

(B) 물론, 나는 할 수 있어.

(C) 미안, 그건 아니야.

(D) 아니, 너는 그렇지 않을 거야.

풀이 상대의 휴대폰을 빌려 쓸 수 있냐는 보기 중 어서 사용하라고 말하는 것이 가장 자연스러우므로 답은 (A)이다.

10. Boy: What is your address?

Girl: ________________

(A) It's 3445-8998.

(B) It's 32 Bay Avenue.

(C) It's April 12th.

(D) It's at 9:45.

해석 소년: 주소가 뭐야?

소녀: ________________

(A) 그건 3445-8998이야.

(B) 그건 32 Bay가야.

(C) 4월 12일이야.

(D) 그건 9:45분에 해.

풀이 주소를 물었으므로 보기 중 가장 적절한 답은 (B)이다.

Part C. Listen and Retell (p.114)

11. Boy: Can we watch a different show?

Girl: No, this show is very interesting.

Question: Where are they?

(A)

해석 소년: 우리 다른 프로그램을 봐도 될까?

소녀: 아니, 이 프로그램 매우 흥미롭다.

질문: 그들은 어디에 있습니까?

풀이 TV를 보고 있는 남녀 그림 (A)가 답이다.

12. Girl: Oh no! The puppy fell into the pool!

Boy: I'll get him!

Question: Who fell into the pool?

(C)

해석 소녀: 이런! 강아지가 수영장에 빠졌어!

소년: 내가 잡을게!

질문: 누가 수영장에 빠졌습니까?

풀이 강아지가 수영장에 빠졌으므로 답은 (C)이다.

13. Boy: What time is the basketball game?

Girl: It's at 7:30 tonight.

Question: When is the basketball game?

(D)

해석 소년: 농구 게임이 몇 시야?

소녀: 오늘 밤 7시 30분이야.

질문: 농구 게임이 언제입니까?

풀이 농구 게임이 7시 30분이라고 했으므로 답은 (D)이다.

14. Girl: Tom, are you sleeping?

Boy: Huh? Oh, sorry about that.

Question: What was the boy doing?

(A) lying

(B) sleeping

(C) laughing

(D) studying

해석 소녀: Tom, 자고 있니?

소년: 응? 아, 미안해.

질문: 소년은 무엇을 하고 있었습니까?

(A) 누워 있기

(B) 잠자기

(C) 웃기

(D) 공부하기

풀이 소년은 잠을 자고 있었으므로 답은 (B)이다.

15. Boy: Where's your brother?

Girl: He's practicing the piano at home.

Question: What is the girl's brother doing?

(A) playing at the playground

(B) playing the piano at home

(C) practicing the flute at home

(D) taking a piano lesson at school

해석 소년: 네 남동생 어디 있니?

소녀: 그는 집에서 피아노를 연습하고 있어.

질문: 소녀의 남동생은 무엇을 하고 있습니까?

(A) 놀이터에서 놀기

(B) 집에서 피아노 치기

(C) 집에서 플룻 연습하기

(D) 학교에서 피아노 수업 받기

풀이 남동생은 집에서 피아노를 연습하고 있으므로 답은 (B)이다.

Words and Phrases practice 연습하다

16. Girl: Susan will meet us at the library.

Boy: Okay, let's take the bus there.

Question: How will they get to the library?

(A) by subway

(B) by bike

(C) by bus

(D) by car

해석 소녀: Susan이 우리를 도서관에서 만날 거야.

소년: 그래, 거기 버스타고 가자.

질문: 그들은 도서관에 어떻게 갈 것입니까?

(A) 지하철로

(B) 자전거로

(C) 버스로

(D) 차로

풀이 소년과 소녀는 버스를 타고 간다고 했으므로 답은 (C)이다.

17. Boy: Don't you want to play computer games?
Girl: Yes, but I have to do my homework first.
Question: Why will the girl NOT play computer games?
(A) She has to do homework.
(B) She has to clean her room.
(C) She has to help her parents.
(D) She has to go to class.

해석 소년: 컴퓨터 게임을 하고싶지 않니?
소녀: 응, 하지만 난 숙제를 먼저 해야 해.
질문: 왜 소녀는 컴퓨터 게임을 하지 않을 것입니까?
(A) 그녀는 숙제를 해야 한다.
(B) 그녀는 방을 치워야 한다.
(C) 그녀는 부모님을 도와야 한다.
(D) 그녀는 수업을 가야 한다.

풀이 숙제를 해야 해서 게임을 하지 않을 것이므로 답은 (A)이다.

[18–19]
Girl: My uncle gave me a digital camera. It was a birthday present. Today, I went to the park and took a picture of a duck. Next, I took a picture of a beautiful tree. Then, I took a picture of some people. Finally, I took pictures of some flowers.

18. Who gave the girl a camera?
(A) her parents
(B) her grandparents
(C) her aunt
(D) her uncle

19. What did the girl take pictures of last?
(A) a tree
(B) a duck
(C) some people
(D) some flowers

해석 소녀: 삼촌이 나에게 디지털 카메라를 주셨다. 이것은 생일 선물이었다. 오늘 나는 공원에 가서 오리 사진을 찍었다. 다음으로, 나는 아름다운 나무 사진을 찍었다. 그리고 나서, 어떤 사람들의 사진을 찍었다. 마지막으로, 나는 꽃 사진을 찍었다.

18. 누가 소녀에게 카메라를 주었습니까?
(A) 그녀의 부모님
(B) 그녀의 조부모님
(C) 그녀의 고모
(D) 그녀의 삼촌

19. 소녀가 마지막으로 찍은 것은 무엇입니까?
(A) 나무
(B) 오리
(C) 사람들
(D) 꽃들

풀이 삼촌이 디지털 카메라를 주었다고 했으므로 18번의 답은 (D)이다. 소녀는 마지막으로 꽃 사진을 찍었으므로 19번의 답은 (D)이다.

[20–21]
Boy: Every Friday evening is family movie night. We order pizza. My brother and I have ham and pineapple pizza. My parents have potato and cheese pizza. We also order chicken wings. Last Friday, we watched a scary movie. I liked it, but my brother did not.

20. What kind of pizza do the boys eat?
(A) ham and pineapple
(B) potato and pineapple
(C) potato and cheese
(D) chicken and cheese

21. Who did NOT like the movie?
(A) the boy
(B) the boy's brother
(C) the boy's mother
(D) the boy's father

해석 소년: 매 금요일 저녁은 가족 영화의 밤이다. 우리는 피자를 시킨다. 남동생과 나는 햄과 파인애플 피자를 먹는다. 부모님은 감자와 치즈 피자를 드신다. 우리는 또한 닭날개를 주문한다. 저번주 금요일, 우리는 무서운 영화를 봤다. 나는 좋았지만, 남동생은 그렇지 않았다.

20. 소년들은 어떤 종류의 피자를 먹습니까?
(A) 햄과 파인애플
(B) 감자와 파인애플
(C) 감자와 치즈
(D) 치킨과 치즈

21. 누가 영화를 좋아하지 않았습니까?
(A) 소년
(B) 소년의 남동생
(C) 소년의 어머니
(D) 소년의 아버지

풀이 소년들은 햄과 파인애플 피자를 먹는다고 했으므로 20번의 답은 (A)이다. 소년의 남동생은 영화를 좋아하지 않았다고 했으므로 21번의 답은 (B)이다.

Words and Phrases order 주문하다

[22–23]
Girl: Chaser is a very smart dog. She lives in the United States. Chaser knows the names of 1,002 things. It took 3 years to teach her all those words. Puck is also a very smart animal, but he is a bird. Puck knows over 1,728 words. Animals are smarter than I thought!

22. How long did it take for Chaser to learn over 1,000 words?

(A) 1,728 days
(B) 1,022 days
(C) 3 months
(D) 3 years

23. What kind of animal is Puck?
(A) a dolphin
(B) a bird
(C) an elephant
(D) a dog

해석 소녀: Chaser은 매우 똑똑한 개다. 그녀는 미국에 산다. Chaser은 1002개의 물건의 이름을 안다. 그녀에게 그 모든 단어들을 가르치는 것은 3년이 걸렸다. Puck도 매우 똑똑한 동물인데 그는 새다. Puck은 1728개 이상의 단어를 안다. 동물들은 내가 생각했던 것보다 똑똑하다!

22. Chaser가 1000개 이상의 단어를 배우는 데 얼마나 걸렸습니까?
(A) 1728일
(B) 1022일
(C) 3개월
(D) 3년

23. Puck은 어떤 종류의 동물입니까?
(A) 돌고래
(B) 새
(C) 코끼리
(D) 개

풀이 1002개의 모든 단어를 배우는 데 3년이 걸렸다고 했으므로 22번의 답은 (D)이다. Puck은 새라고 했으므로 23번의 답은 (B)이다.

[24–25]
Boy: Yesterday we had a talent show at school. I sang a song. I wrote the song myself. John danced hip hop. He is a really good dancer. Kate and Susan played their instruments. Kate played the violin, and Susan played the cello. They did a great job.

24. What did John do at the talent show?
(A) sing
(B) dance
(C) play the cello
(D) play the violin

25. Who played music together?
(A) the boy and John
(B) the boy and Kate
(C) Kate and Susan
(D) John and Susan

해석 소년: 어제 우리는 학교에서 탤런트 쇼를 했다. 나는 노래를 불렀다. 나는 노래를 직접 썼다. John은 힙합을 췄다. 그는 정말 춤을 잘 춘다. Kate와 Susan은 그들의 악기를 연주했다. Kate는 바이올린을 켜고 Susan은 첼로를 켰다. 그들은 훌륭했다.

24. John은 탤런트 쇼에서 무엇을 했습니까?
(A) 노래하기
(B) 춤추기
(C) 첼로 연주
(D) 바이올린 연주

25. 누가 음악을 같이 연주했습니까?
(A) 소년과 John
(B) 소년과 Kate
(C) Kate와 Susan
(D) John과 Susan

풀이 탤런트 쇼에서 노래를 불렀다고 했으므로 24번의 답은 (B)이다. Kate와 Susan이 악기를 연주했으므로 25번의 답은 (C)이다.

Words and Phrases talent show 탤런트 쇼 instrument 악기
talent 재능

Part D. Listen and Speak (p.118)

26. Boy: What can I put in the fruit salad?
Girl: How about some oranges?
Boy: Good. And I'll add apples and bananas.
Girl: ____________________
(A) But I don't like apples.
(B) But you can't cook.
(C) That's very funny.
(D) That's too spicy.

해석 소년: 과일 샐러드에 무엇을 넣을 수 있을까?
소녀: 오렌지는 어때?
소년: 좋아. 나는 사과와 바나나를 추가할게.
소녀: ____________________
(A) 하지만 나는 사과를 좋아하지 않아.
(B) 하지만 너는 요리를 못해.
(C) 그거 되게 재미있다.
(D) 그거 너무 매워.

풀이 사과를 추가한다는 소년의 말에 적절한 소녀의 반응은 (A)이다.

Words and Phrases spicy 매운

27. Boy: What happened to your knee?
Girl: I fell down on the street.
Boy: You should wash the cut.
Girl: ____________________
(A) Okay, I will.
(B) I caught a cold.
(C) Yes, you're clean.
(D) I'll call the doctor.

해석 소년: 무릎 왜그래?
소녀: 길거리에서 넘어졌어.
소년: 상처를 씻어야겠다.
소녀: ____________________
(A) 그래, 그렇게 할게.
(B) 나 감기 걸렸어.
(C) 응, 너는 깨끗해.
(D) 의사한테 전화할게.

풀이 소년의 충고에 대한 적절한 반응은 (A)이다.

28. Girl: Excuse me? Where is the library?
Boy: It's at the end of the hall.
Girl: Thank you.
Boy: ________________

(A) That's good to know.
(B) Great idea!
(C) No problem.
(D) Sure, why not?

해석 소녀: 실례합니다. 도서관이 어디에 있나요?
소년: 복도 끝에 있어요.
소녀: 감사합니다.
소년: ____________
(A) 알기 좋은 정보네요.
(B) 좋은 생각이에요!
(C) 천만에요.
(D) 당연하지, 왜 아니겠어요?

풀이 고맙다는 소녀의 말에 문제될 것 없다는 (C)가 가장 적절하다.

Words and Phrases hall 복도 no problem (부탁 • 질문에 대해) 그럼요, 전혀 문제 되지 않아요. (고마움 • 미안함을 나타내는 말에) 괜찮아요, 천만에요

29. Boy: Why is your face so red?
Girl: I ran all the way to school.
Boy: Why did you do that?
Girl: ________________

(A) I was tired.
(B) I was late.
(C) I was loud.
(D) I was ready.

해석 소년: 얼굴이 왜 그렇게 빨개?
소녀: 학교 오는 길 내내 뛰어왔어.
소년: 왜 그랬어?
소녀: ________________
(A) 나는 피곤했어.
(B) 나는 늦었었어.
(C) 나는 시끄러웠어.
(D) 나는 준비가 되었었어.

풀이 학교 오는 길 내내 뛴 이유를 설명해야 하므로 답은 (B)이다.

Words and Phrases all the way to ~오는 길 내내

30. Girl: What will you do after school?
Boy: I'll have a dance lesson.
Girl: What kind of dance?
Boy: ________________

(A) It's at 4:00.
(B) It's far from here.
(C) It's ballet.
(D) It's very fun.

해석 소녀: 방과 후에 뭐 할거야?
소년: 춤 수업을 할 거야.
소녀: 어떤 종류의 춤?
소년: ________________
(A) 4시에 있어.
(B) 여기서 멀어.
(C) 발레야.
(D) 매우 재미있어.

풀이 춤 종류로 답해야 하므로 답은 (C)이다.

SECTION II READING AND WRITING

Part A. Sentence Completion (p.121)

1. A: Which kite in the sky is yours?
B: ____________ red one is mine.

(A) There
(B) That
(C) These
(D) Those

해석 A: 하늘의 어떤 연이 네 것이니?
B: **저** 빨간 것이 내 것이야.
(A) 저기에
(B) 저
(C) 이것들
(D) 저것들

풀이 '저'라는 뜻의 지시형용사가 필요하고, 단수 형태여야 하므로 답은 (B)이다.

2. A: What did your father say?
B: He ____________ me to study harder.

(A) asked
(B) ask
(C) asking
(D) to ask

해석 A: 아버지가 뭐라고 하셨어?
B: 그는 더 열심히 공부하라고 **부탁하셨어.**
(A) 부탁했다
(B) 부탁하다
(C) 부탁하기
(D) 부탁하기

풀이 did로 물어보았으므로 과거형으로 대답한 (A)가 적절하다.

Words and Phrases harder 더 열심히

3. A: Is Jeff still ____________?
B: Yes, let's go wake him up.

(A) sleep
(B) sleeping
(C) will sleep
(D) to sleeping

해석 A: Jeff 아직도 **자니?**
B: 응, 가서 깨우자.
(A) 자다
(B) 자고 있는
(C) 잘 것이다
(D) 틀린 표현

풀이 'still'은 '여전히, 아직도'라는 뜻의 부사이므로 뒤에 현재형 또는 진행형이 와야 한다. be동사 의문문이므로 빈칸에는 진행형 'sleeping'이 오는 것이 적절하다. 따라서 답은 (B)이다.

4. A: _________ did you buy that ring?
B: Two days ago.
(A) Why
(B) How
(C) When
(D) What

해석 A: 그 반지 **언제** 샀니?
B: 이틀 전에.
(A) 왜
(B) 어떻게
(C) 언제
(D) 무엇

풀이 B의 대답을 보면 시기와 관련된 내용으로 언제를 물어보는 의문사 when이 와야 한다. 따라서 답은 (C)이다.

5. A: We don't have _________ time.
B: Let's hurry.
(A) few
(B) many
(C) much
(D) little

해석 A: 우리 시간이 **많지** 않아.
B: 서두르자.
(A) 거의 없는
(B) 많은
(C) 많은
(D) 거의 없는

풀이 'time'은 셀 수 없는 명사로 앞에 'much' 혹은 'little'이 올 수 있다. 문맥상 시간이 없으니 서두르자는 의미로 (C)가 적절하다. 'many'와 'few'는 뒤에 셀 수 있는 명사가 온다.

Part B. Situational Writing (p.122)

6. Her pockets are _________________.
(A) on the knees of her pants
(B) on the back of her pants
(C) on the sides of her jacket
(D) on the front of her skirt

해석 그녀의 주머니는 **치마 앞에 있다.**
(A) 바지의 무릎에
(B) 바지의 뒤에
(C) 재킷 옆에
(D) 치마 앞에

풀이 주머니는 소녀의 치마 앞에 있으므로 답은 (D)이다.

7. The man is _________________.
(A) swimming in the water
(B) jumping over the waves
(C) running out of the ocean
(D) sitting on the beach

해석 남자가 **바다에서 달려나가고** 있다.
(A) 물에서 수영한다
(B) 파도를 넘어 뛴다
(C) 바다에서 달려나간다
(D) 해변에 앉아있다

풀이 그림에서 남자가 바다 쪽의 반대 방향으로 달려가고 있으므로 보기 중 가장 적절한 답은 (C)이다.

Words and Phrases run out of ~로 부터 달아나다

8. The woman is _________________.
(A) crying into a tissue
(B) reading a book
(C) setting the table
(D) blowing her nose

해석 여자는 **휴지에 얼굴을 묻고 울고있다.**
(A) 휴지에 얼굴을 묻고 울다
(B) 책을 읽다
(C) 식탁(밥상)을 차리다
(D) 코를 풀다

풀이 여자는 휴지에 얼굴을 묻고 울고 있으므로 답은 (A)이다.

Words and Phrases cry into ~에 얼굴을 묻고 울다

9. The mother feels _____________.
(A) angry
(B) happy
(C) sleepy
(D) worried

해석 엄마는 **걱정하고** 있다.
(A) 화난
(B) 행복한
(C) 졸린
(D) 걱정하는

풀이 엄마가 아픈 아이를 안고 병원을 떠올리고 있으므로 답은 (D)이다.

10. The firefighter is saving the cat _________________.
(A) from the top of the tree
(B) from under the tree
(C) from beneath the tree
(D) from out of the tree

해석 소방관이 고양이를 **나무 꼭대기로부터** 구하고 있다.
(A) 나무 꼭대기로부터
(B) 나무 아래로부터
(C) 나무 밑으로부터
(D) 나무 밖으로부터

풀이 그림에서 소방관이 나무 꼭대기에 있는 고양이를 구하고 있으므로 답은 (A)이다.

Part C. Practical Reading and Retelling (p.124)

[11-12]

11. Who will bring chicken wings?
    (A) Loretta and Bobby
    (B) Maya and Jason
    (C) Brenda and David
    (D) Peter and Tom

12. Which things will only one person be bringing?
    (A) forks and spoons
    (B) cups and plates
    (C) vegetables and cookies
    (D) pizza and chicken

해석

발렌타인 데이 파티 등록	
파티에 어떤 음식을 가져올 것입니까? 음식 항목 옆에 이름을 쓰세요.	
음식	이름
야채 요리	Maya, Jason
피자	Peter, Tom
닭날개	Brenda, David
쿠키	Loretta, Bobby
주스와 컵	Doug, James
접시, 포크, 숟가락	Susan

11. 누가 닭날개를 가져올 것입니까?
    (A) Loretta와 Bobby
    (B) Maya와 Jason
    (C) Brenda와 David
    (D) Peter와 Tom

12. 한 사람이 가져오는 것은 어떤 것들입니까?
    (A) 포크와 숟가락
    (B) 컵과 접시
    (C) 야채와 쿠키
    (D) 피자와 닭

풀이 닭날개를 가져오는 것은 Brenda와 David이므로 11번의 답은 (C)이다. Susan이 포크, 접시, 숟가락을 가져오므로 12번의 답은 (A)이다.

[13-14]

13. How long will the walk day last?
    (A) two hours
    (B) six and a half hours
    (C) twelve hours
    (D) twenty-four hours

14. Who will get a prize?
    (A) the fastest walkers
    (B) the farthest walkers
    (C) the healthiest walkers
    (D) the earliest walkers

해석 봄 걷기 대회
언제: 4월 23일 토요일, 오전 6:30 – 오후 6:30
어디: Markham 광장 산책로, 240 John 거리
우리와 같이 해요! 당신이 얼마나 멀리 걸을 수 있는지 보세요.
가장 멀리 걷는 사람들은 상을 받습니다.
즐겁게, 건강하게 지내세요!

13. 걷기 대회는 얼마나 길게 진행됩니까?
    (A) 2시간
    (B) 6시간 반
    (C) 12시간
    (D) 24시간

14. 누가 상을 받을 것입니까?
    (A) 가장 빠르게 걷는 사람
    (B) 가장 멀리 걷는 사람
    (C) 가장 건강한 걷는 사람
    (D) 가장 이른 걷는 사람

풀이 오전 6시 30분부터 오후 6시 30분까지이므로 총 12시간이다. 따라서 13번의 답은 (C)이다. 상을 받는 것은 가장 멀리 걷는 사람이므로 14번의 답은 (B)이다.

Words and Phrases track (사람들이 걸어다녀서 생긴) 길

[15–16]

	Haircut	Shampoo	Blow-dry
Men	$15.00	$5.00	$3.00
Women	$20.00	$5.00	$5.00
Children	$10.00	$3.00	$3.00

15. How much is it for a children's haircut?

(A) $10.00
(B) $13.00
(C) $15.00
(D) $16.00

16. What can a woman get for thirty dollars?

(A) only a haircut
(B) only a shampoo
(C) only a haircut and blow-dry
(D) a haircut, shampoo, and blow-dry

해석 헤어 스타일링 가격

	헤어컷	샴푸	드라이
남자	15달러	5달러	3달러
여자	20달러	5달러	5달러
아이	10달러	3달러	3달러

15. 아이들의 헤어컷은 얼마입니까?

(A) 10달러
(B) 13달러
(C) 15달러
(D) 16달러

16. 여자는 30달러로 무엇을 할 수 있습니까?

(A) 헤어컷만
(B) 샴푸만
(C) 헤어컷과 드라이만
(D) 헤어컷, 샴푸, 드라이

풀이 아이의 헤어컷은 10달러이므로 15번의 답은 (A)이다. 여자의 헤어컷이 20달러, 샴푸가 5달러, 드라이가 5달러이므로 30달러로는 다 할 수 있다. 따라서 16번의 답은 (D)이다.

[17–18]

Place	Name	Country	Points
1st	Patrick Chan	Canada	239.52
2nd	Nobunari Oda	Japan	236.52
3rd	Adam Rippon	United States	233.04
4th	Kevin Reynolds	Canada	218.65

17. How many points did the American get?

(A) 239.52
(B) 236.52
(C) 233.04
(D) 218.65

18. Who came in second place?

(A) Kevin Reynolds
(B) Nobunari Oda
(C) Patrick Chan
(D) Adam Rippon

해석 남자 피겨스케이팅 대회 점수

순위	이름	국가	점수
1등	Patrick Chan	캐나다	239.52
2등	Nobunari Oda	일본	236.52
3등	Adam Rippon	미국	233.04
4등	Kevin Reynolds	캐나다	218.65

17. 미국인의 점수는 몇 점입니까?

(A) 239.52
(B) 236.52
(C) 233.04
(D) 218.65

18. 2등을 한 사람은 누구입니까?

(A) Kevin Reynolds
(B) Nobunari Oda
(C) Patrick Chan
(D) Adam Rippon

풀이 미국인 Adam Rippon은 233.04점을 받았으므로 17번의 답은 (C)이다. Nobunari Oda가 2등을 했으므로 18번의 답은 (B)이다.

[19–20]

How to Make Eggshell Chalk

This chalk is for sidewalk drawing. Do not use it for chalkboards.
You will need: * the shells of 6 eggs
**   * 1 spoon of hot water**
**   * 1 spoon of flour**
**   * food coloring**

Break the eggshells to make a powder.
Put 1 spoon of powder in a cup.
Add the flour and hot water. Then, add food coloring.
Shape it into a stick. Let it dry for 3 days.

19. What is this chalk for?
(A) drawing on windows
(B) drawing on chalkboards
(C) drawing on streets
(D) drawing on paper

20. What do you add last to the eggshell powder?
(A) water
(B) flour
(C) eggs
(D) food coloring

해석 계란 껍질 분필을 만드는 방법
이 분필은 보도에 그리는 용입니다. 칠판에 쓰지 마세요.
당신은 이것이 필요합니다 :
* 계란 6개 껍질
* 뜨거운 물 1 숟가락
* 밀가루 1 숟가락
* 식용 색소
가루로 만들기 위해 계란 껍질을 다 깨세요.
컵에 파우더 한 스푼을 넣으세요.
밀가루와 뜨거운 물을 넣으세요. 그리고, 식용 색소를 넣으세요.
막대기 모양으로 만드세요. 3일동안 마르도록 두세요.

19. 이 분필은 무엇을 위한 것입니까?
(A) 창문에 그리기
(B) 칠판에 그리기
(C) 길거리에 그리기
(D) 종이 위에 그리기

20. 계란 껍질 가루에 마지막으로 넣는 것은 무엇입니까?
(A) 물
(B) 밀가루
(C) 계란
(D) 식용 색소

풀이 이 분필은 보도에 그리는 용도라고 했으므로 19번의 답은 (C)이다. 마지막에 식용 색소를 넣고 모양을 잡으므로 20번의 답은 (D)이다.

Words and Phrases sidewalk 보도, 인도 eggshell 계란 껍질 chalk 분필 flour 밀가루 food coloring 식용색소

Part D. General Reading and Retelling (p.129)

[21–22]
Burj Khalifa is the world's tallest building. It was built in Dubai, United Arab Emirates. It took 5 years and 6 months to build it. The tower opened on January 4th, 2010. The tower is 828 meters tall. It has 163 floors. It takes about one minute to reach the top riding the elevator.

21. How tall is Burj Khalifa?
(A) 101 meters
(B) 163 meters
(C) 509 meters
(D) 828 meters

22. When did work start to build Burj Khalifa?
(A) in 2004
(B) in 2006
(C) in 2008
(D) in 2010

해석 부르즈 칼리파는 세계에서 가장 높은 건물이다. 이것은 아랍 에미리트의 두바이에 지어졌다. 짓는데 5년 6개월이 걸렸다. 이 타워는 2010년 1월 4일에 열었다. 이 타워는 828미터이다. 163개의 층을 가지고 있다. 엘리베이터를 타고 꼭대기로 가는 데는 1분 정도 걸린다.
21. 부르즈 칼리파는 얼마나 높습니까?
(A) 101미터
(B) 163미터
(C) 509미터
(D) 828미터

22. 부르즈 칼리파를 언제 짓기 시작했습니까?
(A) 2004년
(B) 2006년
(C) 2008년
(D) 2010년

풀이 부르즈 칼리파는 828미터라고 했으므로 21번의 답은 (D)이다. 2010년에 완공되었고 총 5년 6개월이 걸렸다고 했으므로 2004년에 짓기 시작했음을 알 수 있다. 따라서 22번의 답은 (A)이다.

[23–24]
The Sun is a middle-aged star. It is the closest star to the Earth. It is 150 million kilometers from the Earth. Alpha Centauri is the next closest star. Sunlight takes just over eight minutes to reach us, but light from Alpha Centauri takes about four years to reach us.

23. How long does it take for light to reach Earth from Alpha Centauri?
(A) about 4 minutes
(B) about 8 minutes

(C) about 4 years

(D) about 8 years

24. What is Alpha Centauri?

(A) the Sun

(B) a moon

(C) a planet

(D) a star

해석 태양은 중년기의 별이다. 이것은 지구와 가장 가까운 별이다. 지구에서 1.5억km 떨어져있다. 알파 센타우리는 그 다음으로 가까운 별이다. 태양 빛이 우리에게 오는 데는 8분 약간 넘게 걸리지만, 알파 센타우리에서 오는 빛은 4년 정도 걸린다.

23. Alpha Centauri에서 빛이 지구에 도달하는데 얼마나 걸립니까?

(A) 약 4분

(B) 약 8분

(C) 약 4년

(D) 약 8년

24. Alpha Centauri는 무엇입니까?

(A) 태양

(B) 달

(C) 행성

(D) 별

풀이 Alpha Centauri의 빛이 지구에 도달하는데 4년 정도 걸린다고 했으므로 23번의 답은 (C)이다. Alpha Centauri는 태양 다음으로 지구에 가까운 별이라고 했으므로 24번의 답은 (D)이다.

Words and Phrases planet 행성 million 백만

[25–26]

Sophie Tucker is a gray and black dog. One day Sophie fell off her family's boat. There were many sharks in the ocean, but Sophie was okay. She swam ten kilometers to a small island. She lived there for four months. Finally, someone saw her and helped her. Sophie is now back with her family.

25. Where did Sophie Tucker live for 4 months?

(A) at her family's home

(B) on an island

(C) on a boat

(D) in the ocean

26. How did Sophie Tucker get back home?

(A) She swam home.

(B) She walked home.

(C) Someone helped her.

(D) Her family found her.

해석 Sophie Tucker은 회색 그리고 검은색으로 이루어진 개다. 어느날 Sophie는 가족의 보트에서 떨어졌다. 바다에는 상어가 많았지만, Sophie는 괜찮았다. 그녀는 작은 섬으로 10km를 수영했다. 그녀는 거기에서 4개월을 살았다. 마침내, 누군가 그녀를 보았고 도와주었다. Sophie는 이제 그녀의 가족의 품으로 돌아왔다.

25. Sophie Tucker은 4개월 동안 어디 살았습니까?

(A) 가족의 집에서

(B) 섬에서

(C) 보트 위에서

(D) 바다에서

26. Sophie Tucker은 어떻게 집에 돌아갔습니까?

(A) 그녀는 집에 헤엄쳐 갔다.

(B) 그녀는 집에 걸어갔다.

(C) 누군가 그녀를 도와주었다.

(D) 그녀의 가족이 찾았다.

풀이 작은 섬에서 4개월을 살았다고 했으므로 25번의 답은 (B)이다. 누군가 그녀를 보고 도와주었다고 했으므로 26번의 답은 (C)이다.

Words and Phrases shark 상어

[27–28]

There are five things I really don't like. Number one: I don't like dropping my ice cream cone. Number two: I don't like visiting the dentist. Number three: I don't like getting a haircut. Number four: I don't like missing the school bus. Number five: I hate smelling my brother's stinky socks.

27. What is something the writer really doesn't like?

(A) missing the subway

(B) cooking meals

(C) visiting the dentist

(D) doing the laundry

28. What is the third thing the writer hates?

(A) getting a haircut

(B) dropping ice cream

(C) smelling stinky socks

(D) missing the school bus

해석 내가 정말 좋아하지 않는 다섯 가지가 있다. 첫 번째: 나는 아이스크림 콘을 떨어뜨리는 것을 좋아하지 않는다. 두 번째: 나는 치과에 가는 것을 좋아하지 않는다. 세 번째: 나는 머리를 자르는 것을 좋아하지 않는다. 네 번째: 나는 스쿨버스를 놓치는 것을 좋아하지 않는다. 다섯 번째: 내 남동생의 냄새나는 양말 냄새를 맡는 것을 싫어한다.

27. 작가가 정말 좋아하지 않는 것은 무엇입니까?

(A) 지하철 놓치기

(B) 요리하기

(C) 치과 가기

(D) 빨래하기

28. 작가가 싫어하는 세 번째는 무엇입니까?

(A) 머리 자르기

(B) 아이스크림 떨어뜨리기

(C) 냄새나는 양말 냄새 맡기

(D) 스쿨버스 놓치기

풀이 작가는 치과가는 것을 싫어하므로 27번의 답은 (C)이다. 작가가 세 번째로 싫어하는 것은 머리를 자르는 것이므로 28번의 답은 (A)이다.

Words and Phrases stinky 냄새 나는 dentist 치과 의사 miss 놓치다 laundry 세탁물

[29–30]

Cooks in the Middle Ages had rules about food. They thought people should eat light foods before heavy foods. So, people ate melons or grapes before meat. Then the stomach was ready to eat heavy foods. Cheese was the heaviest food, so people ate it at the end of meals.

29. Which of the following is the "heaviest" food?

(A) watermelon
(B) meat
(C) grapes
(D) cheese

30. Which are NOT light foods?

(A) melons
(B) meats
(C) oranges
(D) grapes

해석 중세의 요리사들은 음식에 대한 규칙이 있었다. 그들은 사람들이 무거운 음식을 먹기 전에 가벼운 음식을 먹어야 한다고 생각했다. 그래서, 사람들은 고기를 먹기 전에 멜론이나 포도를 먹었다. 그 후 위가 무거운 음식을 먹을 준비가 되었다. 치즈는 가장 무거운 음식이어서, 사람들이 식사 마지막에 먹었다.

29. 가장 무거운 음식은 이 중 무엇입니까?
(A) 수박
(B) 고기
(C) 포도
(D) 치즈

30. 가벼운 음식이 아닌 것은 무엇입니까?
(A) 멜론
(B) 고기
(C) 오렌지
(D) 포도

풀이 가장 무거워서 마지막에 먹은 음식은 치즈이므로 29번의 답은 (D)이다. 고기가 무거워서 고기 전에 멜론이나 포도를 먹었다고 했으므로 30번의 답은 (B)이다.

Words and Phrases light 가벼운 heavy 무거운

memo

memo

ITC 국제토셀위원회

TOSEL
실전문제집

BASIC